Coaching with colleagues

Coaching with colleagues

An action guide for one-to-one learning

Erik de Haan
Yvonne Burger

Translated by Sue Stewart
Illustrations by Selma van Vemde

First published in the Netherlands 2004
by Koninklijke Van Gorcum BV

This edition published 2005 by
PALGRAVE MACMILLAN
Houndmills, Basingstoke, Hampshire RG21 6XS and
175 Fifth Avenue, New York, N.Y. 10010
Companies and representatives throughout the world

PALGRAVE MACMILLAN is the global academic imprint of the Palgrave
Macmillan division of St. Martin's Press, LLC and of Palgrave Macmillan Ltd.
Macmillan® is a registered trademark in the United States, United Kingdom and
other countries. Palgrave is a registered trademark in the European Union and
other countries.

ISBN–13: 978–1–4039–4323–1
ISBN–10: 1–4039–4323–0

This book is printed on paper suitable for recycling and made from fully
managed and sustained forest sources. Logging, pulping and manufacturing
processes are expected to conform to the environmental regulations of the
country of origin.

A catalogue record for this book is available from the British Library.

A catalog record for this book is available from the Library of Congress.

10   9   8   7   6   5   4   3   2
14 13 12 11 10 09 08 07

Printed and bound in Great Britain by
Antony Rowe Ltd, Chippenham, Wiltshire

Contents

Figures

Tables

Preface

Coaching with colleagues

The era of coaching with colleagues

A book about learning with colleagues is entirely in keeping with the spirit of our times. Both the nature and role of 'work' have changed radically in the West in recent decades. Where we work can no longer be predicted on the basis of family background and education. How we work changes almost from month to month, if only due to new developments in the field of information and communications technology. What we expect from work is no longer clear either: for most of us, it is not just about earning a living. Work now serves other purposes, for example satisfying our more personal needs (Maslow, 1962) such as recognition, influence, self-expression and self-fulfilment. As a result, we now expect more and more from work and, by the same token, work has come to 'expect' more of us. Our working lives are gradually becoming more exciting and interesting. It is becoming increasingly difficult to take refuge behind unique expertise or customised approaches – instead, we now have to find a tailored solution for every job or client, to show more of our personal side in our work and to make that personal side 'effective'. 'Work' is becoming more like 'school', in two respects:

- In the contemporary sense of school: a place of training and education, a learning environment or study centre. A place we go to seeking self-development and self-fulfilment.
- In the original sense of the Greek *scholè*: leisure, rest, pleasure and, paradoxically enough, free time and ease. A place we go to find ourselves, to reflect and to spend time doing things that really matter to us.

Not surprisingly, more and more people are feeling the need for a sanctuary where they can reflect on their work, and professionals have higher and higher expectations of such a sanctuary. What they want is a good conversation – a conversation that helps them to think things through systematically and understand them better, to reinforce the connection between themselves and their context, and to help them tackle things differently and more effectively the next time. In the same way as Plato elevated dialogue to an art form for the Ancient Greeks, the aim of many modern professionals is to elevate these 'good conversations' to an art form.

Which brings us to *Coaching with Colleagues*, as a sequel to *Learning with Colleagues* (de Haan, 2004). This book is not concerned with performance appraisal, planning or cathartic conversations. Coaching with colleagues goes much further and involves:

- building up a coaching relationship and making it so strong that both parties can say what is really at issue
- paying attention to the link between work issues and the personality of the colleague
- considering fundamentally different working methods and tailoring their contribution to the colleague, issue and context
- being aware of your own strengths, pitfalls and preferred approaches – and knowing what assumptions underpin your coaching style
- exploring and discussing the limits of your effectiveness as a coach, and making this process of exploration and investigation itself part of the helping conversation.

How are you going to stay 'professional', if not by means of 'helping conversations' with fellow professionals? What are you going to learn from as a professional? Training programmes and courses, which you have already completed? Textbooks, which are outdated almost as soon as they reach the shelves? Clients and customers, who often aren't quite sure themselves what questions they want to ask you?

In our view, coaching is both the easiest and the most complex form of learning with colleagues. Easy: after leafing through these pages for even just ten minutes anyone can apply the most basic yet effective of methods (see the techniques in Chapter 6). And difficult: in the narrow confines of the one-on-one conversation, every contribution – indeed every facial expression or minor shift in attention – can send the conversation off in a completely different direction. This, for us, is what makes coaching such a subtle and wide-ranging craft.

In our view, coaching is an activity that fits in with both meanings of 'school': the learning environment and the place of leisure. The pleasure lies in taking a playful approach to serious and dramatic issues and, conversely, in a serious approach to fantasy and play. The learning aspect lies in the fact that coaching has an advantage over many other methods of professional development in that it can be organised with and through colleagues (from inside or outside the organisation), it can take place close to the place of work, and it affords an opportunity for much-needed peace and concentration.

The structure of this book

This book, *Coaching with Colleagues*, consists of three parts:

1. Part I, *Context for coaching*, contains a brief introduction to coaching and explains a number of central concepts ('What are we actually talking about?').
2. Part II, *Approaches to coaching*, examines a number of approaches to coaching in greater depth and provides a link to the main currents of psychotherapeutic thinking ('How do you go about it?').
3. Part III, *Reflection on coaching*, illustrates some of the skills of the coach and considers the context within which coaching often takes place ('Who coaches where?').

Writing this book was a valuable learning process for us, and one which involved a great deal of mutual coaching. Now that the writing is behind us, we notice that many of our pet subjects have found a home in the book. The final result:

- is eclectic, and therefore places a minimum of restrictions on the reader's freedom of choice
- starts from the reader's own coaching practice and the invitation to develop, from a variety of perspectives, a personal approach to coaching
- contains specific checklists and aids as well as references to underlying theory and research
- describes applicable methods and specific, ready-to-use coaching styles
- includes many examples from our own experience of coaching a wide variety of coachees.

Besides the full, cover-to-cover reading that we, of course, heartily recommend, the reader can take other routes through this book:

- Readers who are looking for a brief introduction to the subject of coaching and are keen to hone their own abilities and skills as coaches in an organisational setting can opt for the route via Chapters 1 (definitions of coaching, mentoring, supervision, etc.), 3 (conditions for coaching), 4 (structure of coaching relationships), 12 (capabilities of the coach) and 14 (organisation coaching).
- Readers who wish to deepen and broaden their own practice as a more experienced coach can opt for the route via different approaches, applications and frameworks, i.e. Chapters 2 (layered communication during coaching), 5, 6, 7, 8, 9, 10 and 11 (different coaching approaches and what works for whom) and 15 (limitations of coaching, both internal and external).

- Readers who wish to develop the role of coach in their own organisation, looking at different approaches and the choice between internal or external coaching, can opt for the route via Chapters 1 (differences between coaching, counselling, mentoring and supervision), 5 (different approaches), 11 (choices between different approaches), 13 (impact of coaching on different learning styles and professional careers) and 15 (limitations of coaching, both internal and external).

The authors as mouthpieces

Who are the authors of an action guide to coaching with colleagues? Developers of coaching methods? Innovators in their field? Coaches with a distinguished record of service? That would be nice. The authors of this book see themselves primarily as editors of work done by others, 'mouthpieces' for methods and specialist knowledge which are often as old as the discipline of coaching itself.[1] All of the coaching approaches in this book – other than, perhaps, the IRONIC METHOD which we developed ourselves (see Chapter 9) – have a long history. Our own contribution is to have translated these approaches into simple methods. As often as possible, we include source references to the authors who actually developed the concepts and methods discussed.

While writing this book we were very involved in learning about coaching – through doing it a lot, reading about it and, together with many colleagues, organising seminars on the subject. We would like to thank some of the colleagues who made this possible:

- The business schools Sioo and De Baak for the many opportunities given to us to develop, for the benefit of participants in coaching courses, some of the material for this book. Since 2001 Erik has been involved as a developer and co-trainer of the second module of De Baak's programme *The Professional as Coach*, and Yvonne and Erik together have been developing and facilitating Sioo's professionalisation module *Coaching!* since 2002. Both programmes have been running twice a year for several years now, and are attracting considerable interest. On a more personal note, we would like to thank Debbie Molhuizen and Tamara van Duin (De Baak) and Marguerithe de Man (Sioo) for taking on the management of these programmes.
- Ina Smith and Bill Critchley of Ashridge Consulting and Charlotte Sills of the Metanoia Institute for their 'mentoring' in applying many of the ideas from this book in Ashridge Consulting's programme *Coaching for Organisation Consultants* and for the opportunity to work with

1. Or 'young' in fact, compared with many other fields. Coaching – individual consultation, mentoring and supervision – really became a discipline only in the latter half of the twentieth century.

verbatim reports (see Appendix B) in the Ashridge accreditation process for professional coaches.

- Sarah Beart of Ashridge Consulting for her idea of applying the ladder of inference method within analytic coaching. We have now gained experience with it ourselves, and the LADDER METHOD has found a home in Chapter 8.
- Lorraine Oliver for her patience in looking for quantitative, 'outcome research' articles about coaching, the needle in the proverbial haystack, at which she has been wonderfully successful.
- Our Canadian-Dutch colleague Nico Swaan for countless detailed suggestions for the English translation, many of which made us rewrite the original Dutch text.
- Trevor Ashwin of Curran Publishing Services for exceptionally careful and patient editing, and for coming up with detailed suggestions regarding every single page of the manuscript.
- Our colleagues Charlotte Sills of the Metanoia Institute and Eunice Aquilina of the BBC's Internal Coaching Services for many helpful and supportive comments and suggestions on the first English draft.
- Selma van Vemde for her ability to bring coaching in all its varied forms – and more! – to life in her attractive illustrations.

This book is dedicated to our own coaches with whom we have learned so much: Erik with Ric Oostburg, Gerard Wijers and Anton Obholzer, and Yvonne with Hanneke Elink Schuurman and, last but not least, Peter Janssen.

Erik de Haan and Yvonne Burger
Erik.DeHaan@Ashridge.org.uk
http://home.hetnet.nl/~e.de.haan
Burger@Sioo.nl
www.Sioo.nl

Part I

Context for coaching

Introduction: 'Helping' conversations

We all have experience of conversations that are helpful to us. Conversations in which we can open our hearts, in which we feel truly understood, in which things become clearer, or in which we can hear ourselves think. These are conversations in which we gather the courage to face difficult issues – and which fill us with gratitude towards the people we have been talking to, even though the latter have often done little more than listen and offer a candid opinion. These are conversations in which we ourselves can take centre stage and ponder out loud on our main preoccupations. Such 'helping' conversations have certain features in common, features which we will try to identify and formalise in this part of the book. As an illustration of the form taken by such 'helping' conversations and how they may arise, this first section contains a brief but fairly comprehensive summary of the coaching profession.

Part I consists of four chapters which go together in pairs:

1. Chapter 1 outlines the breadth of coaching, as regards the type of problem and the corresponding coach's role: as mentor, supervisor, consultant, internal and external colleague. We give an initial indication of the limitations of coaching and of the main skills of the coach, subjects to which we return in more detail in Chapters 12 and 15.

2. Chapter 2 outlines the richness of coaching: richness in the subtlety of the communication and richness in the network of interconnections and references within what is expressed. We provide a window onto the contribution made by the coachee, from verbal, explicit input to the conversation, via implicit and non-verbal input, to things of which the coachee is less aware. We also provide a window onto the contribution made by the coach, which ranges from exploring to suggesting and from supporting to confronting.

3. Chapter 3 illustrates the external conditions which are important for coaching conversations, by outlining in chronological order the kind of process the coach and coachee go through together. We give a summary of the basic principles of coaching, from making preparations and structuring the conversation to the ingredients of coaching contracts.

4. Chapter 4 illustrates the internal involvement which is important for the development of a coaching relationship, by outlining in chronological order the way in which the relationship between coach and coachee can develop. This gives a checklist for the registration of a new coachee, a summary of different forms of relationship during coaching, and a list of points for attention when evaluating coaching.

The aim of this first section is therefore to give a straightforward indication of the way in which a cycle of 'helping' conversations can be structured, and what the most striking events and elements within it are. This first section is aimed in principle at every coach and every coachee. As a result, it is rather general and lacking in direction in terms of interventions and approaches. We hope to add sufficient differentiation and depth later, in Parts II and III, to enable the reader to feel more at home as a unique coach or coachee.

1

A wide scope for conversation

What do we mean by coaching?

Coaching is a method of work-related learning which relies primarily on one-to-one conversations. The two colleagues in the coaching conversation have different roles. The coach is focused on facilitating the coachee's learning and development process. As such, the coach's primary concern is that the coachee takes care of him- or herself. The coach may be a more experienced colleague, an outside professional with the same expertise as the coachee, or an outside adviser who is experienced primarily in 'coaching professionals' and is not – and has never been – active in the coachee's field of expertise. Coaching by one's own manager ('coaching leadership') is usually not geared solely towards learning, as in the definition above, in view of the judgmental nature of the managing relationship. In general, 'managing by coaching' means applying coaching techniques in the practice of leadership.

The aim of coaching is to improve the coachee's professionalism by discussing his or her relationship with certain experiences and issues. The coach's intention is to encourage reflection by the coachee, to release hidden strengths and to overcome obstacles to further development. The focus is on topics such as:

- how the coachee works with others
- how the coachee acts in specific situations, such as those involving managing, negotiating, giving advice or exerting influence
- how the coachee handles difficult situations, with colleagues and clients for example
- how the coachee forms judgments and makes decisions.

These topics are linked not only to the content of the specialist area but also to the person and the knowledge and skills at the coachee's disposal, the way in which (s)he acts, forms judgments, and so on. This makes coaching suitable for many different professional roles.

The coaching process roughly consists of the following phases (see also Chapter 3):

1. Intake and establishment of a coaching contract.
2. Building and maintaining the relationship.
3. Raising awareness.
4. Refining the contract.
5. Facilitating change.
6. Integration, review and evaluation.
7. Closure.

The first and sixth of these, those of intake and integration, often take place together with colleagues of the coachee, or with the coachee's manager.

During the coaching conversation the coachee raises issues related to recent experiences, such as experiences and queries relating to:

- leading others, or managing professionals
- drafting and evaluating proposals
- maintaining relationships with clients, customers or colleagues
- rejected proposals
- internal evaluation of services rendered per customer
- external evaluation: gauging customer satisfaction
- advising customers and clients
- handling differences of opinion with direct reports, customers or clients.

The main feature of coaching is therefore that a professional is given an opportunity to reflect, with the coach's assistance, on his or her own actions and thoughts.

A characteristic feature of coaching is that issues arising from the coachee's professional practice always provide the starting point. The conversations are not therapy sessions during which individuals' personalities are delved into deeply. It is useful, however, to consider the way in which the person contributing an issue deals with that issue personally, and to investigate the extent to which aspects of his or her behaviour are causing or prolonging the issue. The conversation can therefore centre on personal performance, but always in the context of practice.

| 1. Questions where content and specialist knowledge are at the centre, in which this knowledge needs to be applied in specific, difficult situations. | 2. Questions with a content-related component, but where the way in which the coachee relates to and handles the content is important. | 3. Questions where personal characteristics of the coachee are at the centre. |

←──────────────────────────────────────→
Range of coaching questions

'Coaching conversations' therefore cover an area similar to peer consultation (see Chapter 2 of *Learning with Colleagues*):

1. Issues where content is at the centre will often relate to unexpected experiences, for example in drafting proposals and giving advice. These are often put forward in terms of 'what' questions: 'What kind of system should I use here?'
2. Issues where the actions of the issue holder and the way in which (s)he handles a problem are central, are often put forward in terms of 'how' questions: 'Will you, as my coach, help me to decide how to do this, or how to tackle this issue?'
3. Issues where the very person raising the issue is at the centre are often put forward in terms of 'what' questions too. 'What kind of assignments suit me?' 'What is it about me that makes me come up against this time and again?' As these are more personal 'what' issues, they can also be put forward as 'who' questions, along the lines of 'Who am I, and what type of work is suitable for me?'

Because there is a personal component, it is important for the coachee to become aware of his or her actions and to consider alternatives open to them. The coach will help in this respect, primarily by clarifying the problem. The coach therefore has a consultative role and aims to support the coachee in developing a personal approach to a personal issue or problem.

Different forms of coaching

Coaching is an 'umbrella' or 'container' term.[1] A variety of forms of facilitation, mentoring and supervision can be differentiated.[2] What these forms

1. To be precise, coaching is both a 'container' and a 'containment' term. Coaching affords scope and containment to a broad variety of issues and concerns. We see coach and coachee as the 'container' and 'contained' within a 'dyadic' relationship (see Chapter 8 and Bion, 1963).
2. When considering the distinction between mentor and coach, it is interesting to look at the original meanings of both words:

   - *Mentor* is introduced in Homer's *Odyssey* as an old friend of the family. The goddess Pallas Athena assumes his form as a disguise in order to help Odysseus' son, Telemachus, find his father. Both Mentor and Athena have wide experience and knowledge of the situation, and advise and assist Telemachus. A typical example of Mentor's coaching style can be found in Book 22: 'Come hither, friend, and stand by me, and I will show thee a thing'. It is astounding how much insight can be gained from the *Odyssey* – one of the oldest works in Western literature, dating to the eighth century BC – about a concept as modern as 'mentoring'!
   - *Coach*, on the other hand, is defined in the dictionary as: 'A large, closed, horse-drawn carriage with four wheels which conveys esteemed individuals from where they were to where they want to be.' The coach is therefore a vehicle, a

Figure 1.1 The coach is at your disposal

of guidance have in common is the fact that they centre on a relationship between a coachee and a coach ('one-to-one') and that that relationship is focused on the coachee's learning in his or her work. Table 1.1 contains an overview of a number of forms of coaching; we should emphasise that the same terms are defined slightly differently in different places.

way of getting from A to B, and not a person who contributes knowledge or experience and gives instructions. In our view, this is the main difference between a mentor and a coach: one is a more experienced professional who contributes her own expertise; the other is an instrument in the coachee's learning who is not necessarily familiar with or experienced in the coachee's field of work. It is interesting that the word 'coach' comes from the name of the Hungarian village Kocs, where in the 15th century AD a distinctive cart was produced. For us the history of the word symbolises the gradual change in our society from craftsmanship to industrial ('railway coach') to knowledge-intensive (educator-coach) to emotionally intelligent production methods.

In this book we assume that mentoring is a special form of coaching. As a result, we do not refer specifically to mentoring, except in Chapter 11 where we cite research by Ragins et al. (2000), which is particularly concerned with the mentoring relationship.

Table 1.1 Forms and levels of coaching

Different forms of coaching	Objective	Target group	Qualifications of coach	Subject matter	Working method	Level (1–10)
Supervision	Becoming more professional	Professionals	Coach is often simultaneously the manager	Specific work-related issues	Prior agreement on number of sessions	1–4
Individual training/ On-the-job training	Reinforcing skills	Anyone	Subject-matter expertise Training expertise	Behaviour and understanding	Learning by doing, transfer of knowledge and feedback. Limited number of sessions	2–5
Mentoring	Guided learning by doing Action learning	Anyone	Subject-matter expertise	Behaviour and understanding	Observation, feedback. Practice in workplace	4–7
Individual advice	Support in problem-solving	Managers	Expertise as a consultant Management experience	Work in relation to the person	Broadening in context (reading, observing)	3–7
Individual consultation	Becoming more professional Reinforcing knowledge, attitude and skills	Professionals	Mature professional	Person in relation to the work	Individual conversations, upon request of the coachee	5–8
Counselling	Personal development Increasing understanding	Anyone	Psychological expertise	The person within the work environment	Prior agreement on number of sessions (minimum 5)	7–10

In Table 1.1, coaching methods are differentiated by objective, target group, subject matter, working method, qualifications of the coach and level of intervention. This final distinction, *level of intervention* (see Chapter 2 of *Learning with Colleagues*), is an important issue in personal guidance. It relates to the degree in which personal characteristics and behaviours of the coachee form a part of the learning process.

The 'depth' of coaching conversations

In general, there is a link between the person who has an issue and the nature of the problem. For example, a given question can be very difficult for one individual to address, while someone else barely registers it or is able to resolve it with no problem. The degree to which a problem affects us, makes us insecure, causes sleepless nights or intrigues us, says something about the problem, of course, but also something about the person who perceives and 'owns' the problem. The following possibilities can be distinguished:

1. Some problems are 'objective' or technical in nature. For example, if someone is having trouble with certain software packages this might relate to resistance to information technology, or simply to a lack of knowledge or skill. Sometimes, therefore, there is simply a need to acquire knowledge or learn a particular skill. Expert advice can provide a solution here.
2. Sometimes, however, acquiring knowledge or learning new behaviour is not enough. There are underlying patterns which suggest that, though this specific problem may be solved, the same problem (possibly in a different form) will reappear the next day. Here it is important to consider not the incident, but the work context and the pattern generated by the incident. This is not always easy, because a feature of such patterns is that they often go unrecognised by the person concerned. Many people have a tendency to define problems as separate from themselves: 'It's not my fault; it's the work environment; it's my colleagues'. Coaching can provide a solution here.
3. Sometimes issues and problems are so personal that a thorough exploration within the context of work and professional experience is insufficient. An individual's abilities and limitations underlie the problems and issues at hand. A characteristic aspect of such problems is that they are experienced as much privately as they are at work. Therapy can provide a solution here.

In coaching, a number of different levels are present simultaneously (a matter also considered in Chapter 2). The focus is not only on the issue raised, and on ways of dealing with it, but also on the patterns underlying such issues. The coach can often choose which of these levels to pursue, or at which level to make a personal contribution. In making that choice, the coach determines to a large extent how the conversation will continue. The

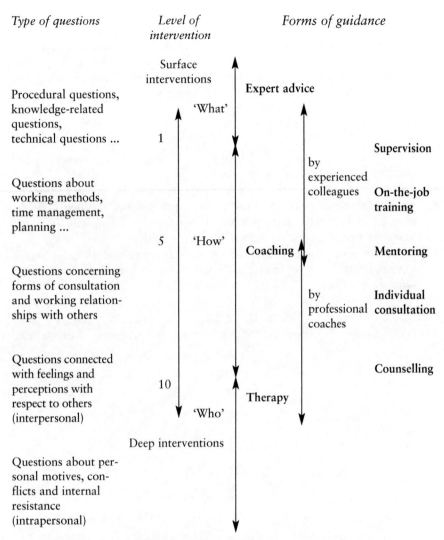

Figure 1.2 The scope of coaching

importance of choosing the 'right' level of intervention therefore often becomes clear only in retrospect.

A much-used summary of levels of intervention is shown in Figure 1.2.

Role and competencies of the coach

The table above makes clear that the demands placed on a coach depend on where the emphasis is placed. An 'all-round' coach understands the main principles of organisation, change and intervention management, and also of clinical psychology. As the depth of intervention increases, the coach must rely increasingly on his or her intuition, psychological understanding and experience, and on 'shadow coaching' by another coach or a peer consultation group. These enable the coach to recognise patterns and mental models, both in the processes described by the coachee and in the meetings between coachee and coach. Bringing these patterns up for discussion can yield significant insights.

Generally speaking, a coach is able to

- identify with the coachee's problem and support the coachee in the search for a solution or an approach,
- encourage the coachee to find new perspectives on his or her problem,
- explore relationships between the problem and the organisational context,
- view his or her own interaction with the coachee as if from the 'outside', and give a transparent account of it when asked,
- relate the issue raised by the coachee to what happens during the coaching conversation, and raise that relationship during the conversation with the coachee.

Part III of this book focuses on the skills a coach can be expected to have, and on the manner in which the coach can bring those different skills to bear.

Summary: a wide scope for conversation

Coaching is a method of work-related learning which relies primarily on one-to-one conversations.

The aim of coaching is to increase the coachee's professionalism by discussing his/her relationship to the experiences and problems raised.

The scope of coaching is fairly wide, embracing:

- Supervision: approach, procedures, results.
- On-the-job training: approach and behaviour.
- Mentoring: approach, forms of consultation and working relationships.
- Individual consultation: the person in relation to work.
- Counselling: the person within the work.

Coaching is therefore situated somewhere between expert advice and therapy, at different levels of intervention.

The main skills required of coaches are:

- Listening skills: identifying with the coachee's problem.
- Intervention management: encouraging the coachee to find new perspectives and solutions.
- Organisation management: exposing links between problem and organisational context.
- Psychological understanding: exploring and raising the coachee's interaction during the conversation.

2
A rich field of exploration

This chapter sets out to provide a clear explanation of the complex and multi-layered nature of coaching conversations. It starts with a window onto the coachee used by both coach and coachee: this is an extended version of the Johari window (see Luft, 1969, or *Learning with Colleagues*, Chapter 10). It then introduces a window onto the coach, which gives an idea of the different emphases that coaches can apply in their approach.

In our experience, coaching conversations are very rich and full conversations. They often deal with issues of real importance to the coachee – issues with a broad background, and issues the coachee has worked on previously, either alone or with friends and colleagues. In addition, the coachee reveals not only something about the issues and situations, in words and in gestures, but also something about themself in the way in which they handle those issues. In the way in which he or she tells a story, the coachee invites the coach to contribute in a specific manner – for example by listening, asking questions, being stern, empathising or lending expertise. Clearly, the attitude of the coach makes a real difference. By the way in which he or she asks questions and listens – and, more generally, by every contribution to the conversation (not contributing is not an option![1]) – the coach influences the conversation both intentionally and unintentionally. An orderly, well-controlled conversation is out of the question – there are simply too many variables. It sometimes feels as if we are 'playing' in a very confined space where every tiny movement, every glance and gesture acquires meaning, a meaning that interacts with other meanings and causes ripples in pre-existing patterns of meaning. For us, coaching conversations are quite literally a 'craft of skill and precision', offering access to an extremely rich field of exploration for those who open themselves up to it. A good coach does precisely that.

Window onto the coachee

In a coaching conversation, both coach and coachee are focused on what is going on in the coachee's mind. They are therefore working together on the

1. See Watzlawick et al. (1967) on the fact that we cannot *not* communicate.

same territory: the 'material' which is the coachee. It is useful to have a 'map' of that territory, or a 'window' onto everything the coachee is contributing to the conversation at each moment. Figure 2.1 is a map of the playing field between coach and coachee, derived from the 'Johari window' (see *Learning with Colleagues*, Chapter 10).[2]

At any one moment in a coaching conversation, coachee and coach are standing side by side on the map and looking out at what is going on within the coachee. This is not a conventional model of communication, with a sender, a receiver and numerous distortions in the communication process (as, for example, in Schulz von Thun, 1982). Such models fall short when it comes to coaching: all too easily we give in to the tendency to experience our communication with other people as our interaction with the things that surround us. Sure enough, 'things' send out 'signals' – and, sure enough, those signals come through clearly or less clearly – and, sure enough, we receive those 'signals', process different aspects of them, construct some sort of internal 'representation' of the things and react to that in turn. Yet this representation does not do full justice to the complexity of our interaction with things, and definitely falls short as a representation of our communication with people, where something fundamentally

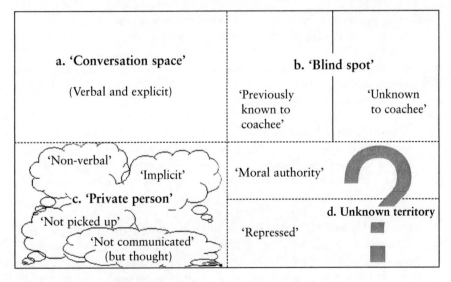

Figure 2.1 The window onto the coachee: the playing field between coach and coachee

2. There are good alternatives to our map, such as the Comparative Script System in Lapworth, Sills and Fish (2000) or the more complex Grid used by Bion (Bion, 1962). The use of one of these maps can be 'liberating' for coaches as they will be able to 'place' new information quickly, thereby freeing themselves for what is to come. Maps also help to summarize what is *not* said, to trace what is perhaps being overlooked both by the coach and by the coachee.

Figure 2.2 Coach and coachee walk side by side on a map provided by the coachee. Together they discover the landscape *and* the map.

different is going on. People literally become absorbed in each other when they communicate, and create a communicative unit (Watzlawick et al., 1967) – even a hermit is not a hermit without the group of people with respect to which (s)he assumes the role of hermit. It is this communicative unit which we attempt to illustrate below. It consists of four 'fields', discussed in the following sections.

a. The conversation space or 'free space'

The *conversation space* is the field worked out in most detail on our map (see Figure 2.3). This represents the explicit and visible part of the coachee's contribution. The coachee's 'story' always has both 'expressive' and 'appellant' aspects simultaneously (Schulz von Thun, 1982):

- *Expressive* describes the part that reveals something about the coachee and their issues. The coachee expresses him- or herself and so provides personal insights. The stories told by the coachee – for example about the background to an issue, or things that have happened this week, are expressive. The opinions, feelings and facts (s)he contributes are also expressive.
- *Appellant* describes the part where the coachee makes an appeal to the coach. In other words, (s)he implicitly or explicitly conveys an expectation or hope of a particular response. At the simplest level the coachee tells his or her story, assuming the coach is listening. Or the coachee asks a question and then usually expects an answer from the coach – unless it is a rhetorical question, when the coachee rather expects agreement from the

coach. Or else the coachee has an overt request for help ('I'd like your opinion on this!'). At a subtler level the appeal may be implicit, as in 'I'm absolutely hopeless at this', which often implies 'will you do it for me?' Appellant behaviour becomes even subtler, and often more interesting for the coaching process itself, when the coachee appeals to the coach for help in a specific way – for example, by pressing for solutions, or by adopting a superior stance.

Expressive and appellant elements of conversations are not easy to distinguish. Most typically expressive comments also have an appellant aspect (for example, 'I think it's a good idea to take another look at that' implies 'and I hope you will go along with me'). Conversely, the most strongly appellant comments also have an expressive significance (for example, 'I would like to hear your opinion about a conversation that I had this week' also communicates 'because I am preoccupied with it at the moment').

Another useful distinction in the conversation space is that between the different *levels* in the conversation, from factual to personal. We normally assume four levels of conversation, or four different levels of explicit communication that qualify each other:

1. Contributions concerning the *content* of the conversation, that is, the story being told by the coachee, and facts and statements (s)he provides. This concerns all sorts of information being conveyed at any particular moment in the conversation. Contributions on this level are often expressive.
2. Contributions concerning the *procedure* of the conversation, in other words, its different stages, structure and working method. This concerns attempts by the coachee to organise the conversation. Contributions at this level are often appellant ('How would you like me to tell my

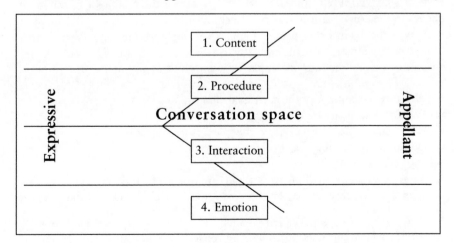

Figure 2.3 The conversation space in the Johari window in more detail

story?'), but are not necessarily so ('First I will talk about the meeting and then I will say something more about my colleague herself').

3. Contributions concerning the *interaction* in the conversation: how the parties to the conversation respond to each other, what roles they adopt and their attitude towards each other.[3] Contributions at this level are often appellant ('Yes, but you are my coach ...'), and can also be partly expressive ('I think we're stuck here ...').

4. Contributions concerning the *emotion* in the conversation, i.e. about feelings currently being experienced by the coachee or coach. Contributions at this level are often largely expressive ('I still feel angry about it now'; 'Your response moves me').

In general, these four levels are easier to distinguish than the expressive and appellant aspects of communication, even if it is not always easy to separate the third and fourth levels (see, for example, the last example under 'emotion', which could also have appeared under 'interaction'!). An important boundary between these levels is that between the first and the other three, between:

- statements concerning the coachee's 'case' (content), and
- statements concerning this conversation, at this moment (procedure, interaction, emotion).

The first level (content) always concerns 'there and then' and the other levels always concern 'here and now' – the procedure now, the interaction now and the feelings now. Other procedures, interactions and feelings remain more remote and cannot be distinguished from the content of the conversation. If a contribution relates to the structure of the conversation, it is purely procedural. If it relates to the way in which the two parties to the conversation respond to each other, it is purely interactive. If it relates to the feelings of individual parties in the conversation, it is purely emotional.

As with the distinction between 'expressive' and 'appellant', it is clear that all four levels are always present implicitly in every conversation. The coachee and coach can answer the four accompanying questions at any moment:

- What is the content of the conversation now?
- What is the structure of the conversation now?
- What is the interaction within the conversation now?
- What are my feelings in this conversation now?

All parts of the conversation space which are not explicitly on the table at this moment and which concern the coachee remain safely hidden in the 'private

3. This aspect of communication is often also classified under the *relationship aspect*, which concerns not only this conversation but also the relationship between coach and coachee more generally (Schulz von Thun, 1982).

person' quadrant in the Johari window, where they await (possible) communication in the future.

b. The private person

In Figure 2.1 (page 15) we drew thought bubbles in this quadrant. Ultimately this quadrant concerns what happens within the coachee during the conversation but is not directly communicated or picked up by the coach. This is therefore the part of the map where the coachee is more at home than the coach. The following levels can be identified in this quadrant, in order of decreasing accessibility to the coach:

1. *Non-verbal information* from the coachee (Mehrabian, 1972), such as:
   - proximity, attitude, movement, gestures and facial expressions
   - intonation, volume, strength and tone of voice
   - interjections such as 'mmm', 'er' and 'um'.

   It is well known that our non-verbal communication conveys an enormous amount of information. In the event of contradictory verbal and non-verbal signals, the non-verbal impression generally appears to be the stronger.[4] Non-verbal information is generally implicit and therefore leaves a lot to intuition and guesswork. As a result, non-verbal communication occurs primarily in the space of the private person.

2. *Implicit information* from the coachee, that is, information which can be read 'between the lines'. This information is again both expressive and appellant. Here too, a wealth of information is expressed through word choice, word repetition, word stress and internal contradictions.[5] In fact, implicit communication forms a grey area between all four quadrants. Think of vague, barely audible words: do they belong to the 'conversation space', or the 'private person' space? Do they reveal something about the coachee in the 'blind spot', or do they make coach and coachee guess about their origin, which means that they remain 'unknown territory'? To a large extent, coaching results in implicit communication of this kind becoming more explicit, and the coachee literally being able to find a place for it.

3. *Information from the coachee that remains unheard*: information which is explicitly communicated by the coachee, but is not picked up or consciously registered by the coach.

4. *Uncommunicated thought* – this is all of the information that the coachee has decided to keep to him- or herself.

4. Mehrabian (1972) – with regard to the communication of 'liking' in words, voice and facial expression – describes how subjects' reactions can be described as $0.07 \times$ (influence of words) $+ 0.38 \times$ (influence of voice expression) $+ 0.55 \times$ (influence of facial expression). The non-verbal signals appear to dominate strongly!

5. The coachee is unaware of much of his/her own implicit information, which therefore then belongs in the 'blind spot'.

5. *Everything that is not currently on the table*: the entire remaining private person of the coachee, including everything (s)he has experienced and is able to retrieve. This field is connected with the unknown territory, which contains all sorts of experiences which the coachee can no longer recall.

Clearly, the 'size' of the private person decreases the more the coachee is prepared to reveal personal details, but also the better the coach is able to register less obvious signals.

c. The blind spot

The blind spot is that part of the coachee (or of his/her contribution) that the coach can observe but that the coachee is unaware of personally. It is therefore the part of the map where the coach is more at home than the coachee. For example, certain emotions may become visible on the face of the coachee; or the coachee may omit certain aspects of a story, or have forgotten them entirely.

This area can be divided into two general areas (Freud, 1923):

1. The part previously known to the coachee, sometimes called the 'preconscious'. The coach has only to mention or recall a fact and the coachee remembers it. An example is the 'homework' for a particular session, with which the session was intended to begin. Imagine that the coachee starts off on a completely different tack. When the coach mentions the homework, a surprised and slightly guilty expression may appear on the coachee's face: an indication in the blind spot that the homework was in his or her preconscious mind.
2. The part unknown to the coachee. The coachee has a lot to learn here, by definition, so the coach can make a valuable contribution by raising aspects from this field in the conversation.

d. Unknown territory

The coachee's 'unknown territory' also contains a 'preconscious' area. This area concerns information which may come to the coachee's attention accidentally and is then recognised as the coachee's reaction shows. This preconscious is connected with the preconscious in the 'blind spot', which is known to the coach, but not to the coachee at this moment.

Leaving aside this 'preconscious' area, the unknown territory is in fact one great unknown: we don't actually know for sure whether there is anything in it. This is where coach and coachee embark on a voyage of discovery together. The area as such remains fundamentally, and by definition, unknown: if coach or coachee are indeed able to say something about it, it appears immediately in one of the other quadrants of the Johari window. However, there are many signs that there is 'something else' in addition to these quadrants, if only because memory ebbs and flows, or because new feelings and ideas sometimes present themselves initially in an incomplete state. The generation of new ideas and the unearthing of memories seem to be based on an activity which itself lies outside our own awareness. Chapter 8 shows that there are many pointers to the existence of a personal 'unknown territory' and that we can find pointers to the existence of this unconscious in our Freudian slips, humour, emotions and dreams. Freud wrote about this at length, and was also bold enough to classify the content of this unknown – and in principle unknowable – zone using the following main distinction (Freud, 1923):

1. The *moral authority* that influences what ends up in the unknown territory, and what can emerge from it. This area consists of the 'unconscious conscience' (an internal representation of 'evil') and the 'ego ideal' ('an internal representation of good') and exercises a sort of controlling influence on memories, utterances and emotions, in terms of what is 'permitted' or 'not permitted'. Freud referred to this as the 'super-ego' (Über-Ich). We believe it is helpful if the coach is aware of the possible existence of a super-ego, which opens the possibility that a coachee is unknowingly not permitting thought about certain things, or does not allow him/herself to find and implement certain solutions.
2. The *hidden or repressed material* itself: the facts, desires, feelings and fantasies being created or dismantled. This material is indeed present but the conscious mind has no access to it, nor is it visible in the coachee's blind spot. Sometimes we are capable of perceiving the existence of something like this within ourselves: for example, while scanning a newspaper or magazine our thoughts may suddenly be drawn to something or someone, but only later do we notice that the relevant name was printed on the very page we were reading. Evidently, we did perceive the key word but did not initially admit it into our conscious mind.

This simple classification of the unknown area can sometimes come in handy. The simultaneous presence of so many fields – in the 'conversation space', the 'private person' and the 'blind spot' as well as in the 'unknown territory', all at the same time – gives an indication of the richness of a coaching conversation at any moment in time. Bear in mind too that the fields also qualify and comment on each other, and it becomes clear that the sheer number of possibilities is incalculable.

An example
A coachee who says 'I have a pain in my big toe' is reporting all of the following simultaneously:

- a fact
- a topic for a conversation

- an implicit qualification which may say something about the seriousness of the conversation
- an implicit relationship definition ('I talk about my pain and you listen')
- an appeal to the coach ('Help me endure my pain!')
- a feeling
- a non-verbal qualification which may say something about the severity of the pain
- the need not to continue with previous topics of conversation
- an expression of him- or herself as coachee.

All of these things come together at the moment of the conversation. The coach has the choice of doing nothing, following up any of these messages, or indeed continuing with or proposing a completely different type of conversation or conversational content. An overwhelming variety of choices.

We hope, of course, that our 'map' has brought some clarity and order to coaching conversations. At the same time, however, such a simple map skims over much of the subtlety, misunderstanding, incomprehension and fantasy that also enter coaching conversations. The different fields in the map often refer to each other, and the coachee's communication may bring together meanings on many levels at the same time (a phenomenon known as 'condensation' – see Malan, 1995). Moreover, the coachee tells personal stories which (s)he has already self-censored to a large extent; these stories lead the coach to think about the coachee in a certain way, again coloured with a mixture of interpretations, self-censorship and misconceptions. One might say that the distortions and misconceptions of the coachee are still somewhere in the 'private person' and that the distortion and (mis-)understanding on the part of the coach lie somewhere in the 'blind spot' – but that too would be to skim over all of the destructiveness and creativity inherent in one-on-one conversations. Our aim has been to show how rich the playing field of coaching is – all the simultaneously present ambiguity and uncertainty simply provide more evidence of that richness!

Window onto the coach

In the coaching conversation the coachee continually produces new information which can find a place somewhere in the Johari window. At the same time, the coach has great freedom in the way (s)he responds to that information. To bring some structure to that freedom, we also offer a window onto the contribution made by the coach. Later, in Part II of this book, we will introduce at least one specific coaching method for each quadrant in this window. We will also examine in greater depth the effects of the different methods, the similarities between the methods, and their correspondence to combinations of coachees and coachee issues.

It is assumed that the coach makes two fundamental contributions:

1. *Direction* of contribution: exploring or suggesting? The coach can choose at each moment to follow and liberate the coachee's thoughts and contributions, or to constrain them and introduce his or her own thoughts and contributions. This enables the coach to influence the direction of the conversation, by deciding whether to 'lead' or to 'follow' the coachee. In the first instance the coach will suggest or propose something; in the second the coach will put him- or herself at the service of a joint exploration or discovery process.

2. *Nature* of contribution: supporting or confronting? The coach can decide at each moment to build on and reinforce the coachee's strengths, or else to bring up the coachee's weaknesses and help him or her overcome them. This enables the coach to influence the construction or deconstruction of the conversation, by deciding to support or challenge the coachee more. In our experience, most coachees expect both support and confrontation from their coaches. The coach can decide when to contribute one or the other.

Figure 2.4 The coach attempts to portray the coachee as faithfully as possible. Coaching means observing with great clarity and then painting in minute detail.

Combining each of these possibilities gives a minimal playing field for the coach encompassing four options:

1. Exploring and supporting, or facilitating the coachee with encouragement and understanding. The coach attempts to explore the issue together with the coachee and contributes warmth and understanding to the conversation. This approach is referred to henceforth as *person-focused*.
2. Exploring and confronting, or facilitating the coachee at a greater distance. The coach attempts to look at what the coachee is leaving out and cannot appreciate personally, thus contributing understanding and objectivity to the conversation. This approach is referred to henceforth as *insight-focused*.
3. Suggesting and confronting, or helping the coachee with suggestions and instructions. The coach attempts to offer the coachee a new framework or approach to the problems being considered, and contributes ideas and recommendations to the conversation. This approach is referred to henceforth as *problem-focused*.
4. Suggesting and supporting, or helping the coachee with options and positive feedback. The coach attempts to send the coachee off on a more positive, constructive train of thought and to help with suggestions for the future. This approach is referred to henceforth as *solution-focused*.

As Figure 2.5 shows, each of the four orientations on the playing field results in a different orientation on the part of the coach.

Interestingly, the orientations in the quadrants, to which we return later (in Chapters 5 and 12), show other familiar polarities which are relevant to coaching:

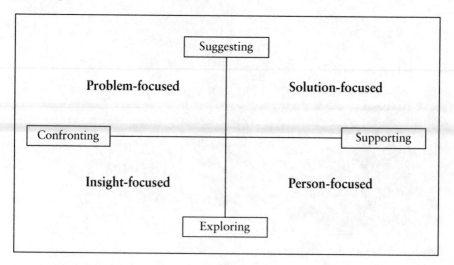

Figure 2.5 The window onto the coach: different contributions from the coach

1. The *level* of addressing coaching issues (from top left to bottom right) – ranging from the coachee's problem to the coachee as a person, from 'what' to 'who' questions, and from superficial to more personal levels of intervention (see Chapter 1). This is a dimension that runs from content to person. The coach makes a choice, with regard to intervention level, by adopting a *problem-focused* or *person-focused* stance.
2. A *time orientation* from past to future (from bottom left to top right) – from the current situation, how it came about and what can be learned from it, to solutions and suggestions for the future. This is a dimension that runs from causes to options. The coach makes a choice, on this time dimension, by adopting an *insight-focused* or *solution-focused* stance.

In Figure 2.6, these intervention levels and time axes have been added.

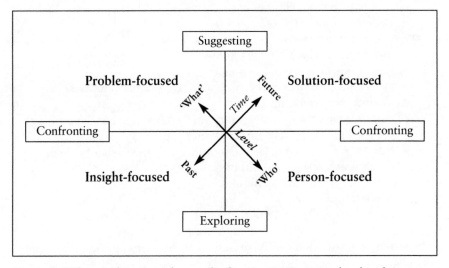

Figure 2.6 The window onto the coach, showing intervention level and time axes

Summary: a rich field of exploration

During coaching conversations, *both* coach and coachee are focused on the coachee's issues.

These conversations are extremely rich and complex in nature, because the coachee offers a great variety of 'material' simultaneously and because all sorts of information and behaviours are interwoven and qualify each other.

The 'material' that is the coachee can be presented with somewhat deceptive clarity using the *Johari window*:

1   The conversation space, containing:
    - expressive and appellant aspects
    - four levels of communication: content, procedure, interaction and emotion.
2. The private person, containing:
    - non-verbal information
    - implicit information
    - information which remains hidden
    - thoughts which are not expressed
    - everything else the coachee might contribute but does not.
3. The blind spot, containing:
    - that of which the coachee is unaware at this moment but of which the coach is aware (the 'preconscious')
    - that of which the coachee is entirely unaware but of which the coach is aware (the actual blind spot).
4. The unknown territory, containing:
    - a moral authority
    - that which is repressed on behalf of the moral authority.

The coach's contribution can be presented clearly using the *window onto the coach*.

1. Person-focused: observing and supporting the coachee from the coachee's perspective.
2. Insight-focused: considering the coachee from an independent perspective.
3. Problem-focused: helping the coachee with an approach to the problem.
4. Solution-focused: supporting the coachee in his/her search for solutions.

3
Structuring the coaching journey

This chapter outlines a number of aspects that we generally attend to at the start of coaching and when structuring our coaching conversations. We give generally applicable suggestions for structuring and conducting the whole process and individual conversations and point out that different approaches to coaching are dictated by different initial conditions. Some coaching approaches can be applied during a stroll with the coachee; for others, taking notes during the conversation is vital. The differences between approaches are dealt with in Part II.

At Ashridge, we usually assume an underlying coaching process which is basically circular, spiralling upwards, and has seven intuitive and sometimes overlapping phases:

1. *Intake and establishment of a coaching contract*
   In every intake there should be some check for boundary issues and conflicts of interest. Coach and coachee clarify their mutual expectations as much as possible. A coaching contract has three areas of significance: administrative, professional and psychological. At the very least, the contract contains a mention of the objectives, the number of sessions (often between five and twenty), the frequency, duration and location of sessions, and the range of learning methods to be utilised.
2. *Building and maintaining the relationship*
   This 'working alliance' means agreement in practice – and not only in the letter of the contract! – about such things as tasks and goals of the coaching relationship, and the establishment of empathy, genuineness and efficacy in the relationship.
3. *Raising awareness*
   Where coach and coachee explore key issues, needs, gaps, patterns and problem triggers. The coaching serves largely to strengthen insight and self-acceptance.

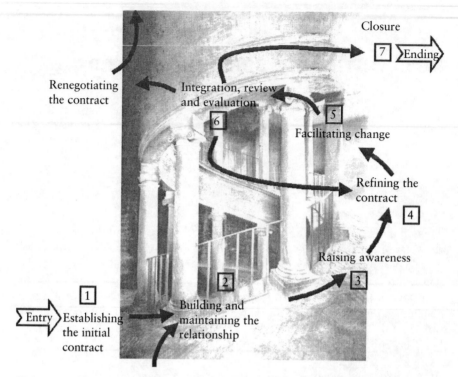

Figure 3.1 The coaching process, as seen through the eyes of the coach: with the help of the famous spiral staircase of Bramante we have tried to express the circular, and at the same time progressive, nature of a coaching journey

4. *Refining the contract*
   Where coach and coachee review the coaching process up to a given point, take stock of the outcome in the light of the original goals, and explore options for the future. This may take place halfway in the coaching journey and may be a moment to liaise with other involved parties.
5. *Facilitating change*
   The coach helps the coachee to build commitment and enthusiasm for practice and experiment.
6. *Integration, review and evaluation*
   Coach and coachee explore together the results of the journey and implications of the outcome. The coachee evaluates the coaching and a decision is taken towards either renegotiating the coaching contract or ending the journey.
7. *Closure*
   Where coach and coachee appreciate their common achievements, perhaps look once more at forestalling relapse and – more or less ceremoniously – make their farewells.

Basic principles

General principles

- The coach and the client are equals (i.e. they are not in a reporting relationship).
- Clients ultimately know best what is good for them and can decide themselves what they do or do not want, both in their private and in their professional life – clients are therefore responsible for the choices that they make and accountable for their actions.
- The responsibility of the coach is to give the client an opportunity to explore, discover and clarify ways of living and working more satisfyingly and resourcefully.
- During coaching the goals, resources and choices of the client have priority over those of the coach.

For the coach

- Individual coaching conversations aim to support the coachee in his or her continued professional development.
- The conversation is shaped by the coachee's learning objectives; however, the coachee remains personally responsible for achieving those objectives.
- The coachee's contribution is the starting point for the conversation, not what the coach thinks the coachee should learn or do.
- Everything the coachee contributes is completely confidential. The person being coached must be able to and dare to be vulnerable.
- Adequate time, peace and quiet are a *sine qua non* for coaching.

For the coachee

- Everything can be raised and subsequently may serve as 'material' in order to explore the coachee's own role and approach.
- Before the start, the coachee concludes a 'contract' with the coach specifying learning objectives, and how they will work together to achieve those objectives. The coachee also agrees the frequency (for example, once a month or every six weeks), the length (for example, an hour and a half) and the number of sessions. After that, coach and coachee decide jointly whether to continue or terminate the sessions, and conclude a new contract if necessary.

Making an appointment and preparations

Conversations are the methodological basis of coaching. The first conversation starts even before it has actually begun. Coach and coachee have expectations, questions, and conscious or unconscious impressions of each other. The first step on the coaching journey has been taken when the coachee decides to enter into a conversation with you here and now.

The first action is usually taken by the coachee, namely making an appointment for a time and a place. A lot can happen during a short telephone conversation. From their interaction with you, you learn something about the coachee's emotional involvement in the issue they wish to address , and how they deal with time and space Sometimes you immediately notice something that will prove later on to be a very significant detail.

Points for attention during such first contact situations include the following:

- Set a time limit for the process, to monitor its effectiveness and to protect the space and focus needed for the conversation.
- On a practical note: take the coachee's telephone number, so you can get back to him or her.

After the first conversation, the coachee will know if there is a 'click' – if there is sufficient contact for you to work together. In addition, coach and coachee will have gained an initial impression of the basic themes. If you think that you are not the most suitable coach for these themes, or for particular coachees, you can still help them by referring them to someone else.

Preparation for a conversation

Novice coaches sometimes have a tendency to want to prepare for a conversation. The risk here is that you will be concerned primarily with your own agenda during the conversation. It is more important to 'empty your mind', so that you can concentrate fully on your coachee, as well as:

- being aware of your own involvement (how do you feel and what does that mean?)
- putting yourself in the role of coach (not colleague, manager, consultant or trainer, for example).

Venue and set-up

The coach is generally the host or hostess. Consider the venue for the coaching. Do you go to the coachee or does (s)he come to you? What are the possible implications of this? In general, the following are recommended:

- some distance from the coachee's workplace: in your office or on neutral territory
- a quiet room with pleasant lighting and atmosphere, where you yourself feel comfortable

- a seating arrangement where you are at an angle to each other, so that the coachee can choose to look away and does not feel put on the spot
- chairs in which you can easily keep your balance.

Ask yourself who is sitting nearest the door and what the implications of this might be.

The following set-up is recommended:

- seating position: 120 degree angle
- table not too large (moveable)
- chairs in which you can relax, but not slouch
- room tidy, well-lit, not too cold.

Starting the conversation

The first five minutes are often critical. There is no such thing as a neutral introduction. The coachee's theme often comes up right at the start of the conversation. The first question should therefore be as open as possible. In his or her first sentences, a coachee often outlines a relevant problem and offers a personal view on it. But this can also happen in *the last five minutes*,

Figure 3.2 The coach organises the most appropriate set-up for the conversation

when the 'door-knob phenomenon' may operate: some people may be unable to say what is really bothering them until the last five minutes, so that they don't have to talk about it any further during this session.

Try to establish why the coachee is coming to you at this point in time with this issue. Be clear and check that the other person understands you. It is not the intention that this conversation should result in further confusion on the part of the coachee.

Taking notes during the conversation has advantages and disadvantages:

Advantages of note-taking	Disadvantages of note-taking
• Helps to focus attention	• Diverts attention from non-verbal information
• Helps to structure the coachee's contribution	• Distances the coach from the coachee
• Helps to prepare for the next conversation	• Provides a form of foothold for the coach that can be deceptive

Often, it comes down to the coach's personal choice: whatever (s)he is more comfortable with. It can also depend on the approach and working method that you choose as coach (see Part II of this book).

Some coaches ask their coachee to make notes during or after the conversation. Similar advantages and possible disadvantages apply here too, this time for the coachee.

Continuing the conversation: the art of listening

Coaching is mainly a matter of listening and asking questions, although a whole range of different interventions also enter into it (summarised in Chapter 12).

The following points are important *when asking questions* (see also Chapter 3 of *Learning with Colleagues*):

- *Open questions* are the most effective way to increase awareness and accountability. Open questions start with 'what', 'when', 'who', 'how many'. 'Why' is not recommended because it often puts others on the defensive. A better approach is to ask questions such as: 'What are your reasons?'; 'In what stages?'; 'What does that achieve?'. Leading questions are not recommended – if you have a suggestion, better to just come out with it.
- In principle, start with *general questions* and concentrate increasingly on *specific details*. This allows you to uncover important (hidden) factors.

The following points are important *when listening*:

- Be aware of the different aspects attached to a message (see previous chapter):
  - the content-related aspect (things, facts, other people)
  - the expressive aspect (own feelings or judgments)
  - the appellant aspect (appeal to the coach to behave in a certain way)
  - the relationship aspect (how the coachee defines the relationship with the coach, for example as a relationship based on trust).

  You can raise these aspects with the help of 'meta-communication'; then the listening moves from the content to the way in which the coachee communicates.
- Listen for intonation and word choice.
- Pay attention to body language.
- Show that you are listening to your coachee by offering small encouragements (gestures, posture, facial expressions) and by following the coachee verbally (in your responses, using the other person's language as much as possible).
- Give back what you hear by mirroring or summarising and checking ('So, if I understand you correctly ... is that right?').
- Bring things back to specifics if the coachee has a tendency to generalise problems (in terms of 'everyone', 'always', 'everywhere', 'never'). Ask for examples, precise details, and so on.
- Reflect the feelings of the coachee by naming them, so that listening becomes more explicit and the coachee also has an opportunity to 'listen to' his or her own emotions.
- Be aware of how you are feeling yourself! Your own feelings may yield additional information about the coachee, but may also affect your impartiality or objectivity.
- Be aware of possible projection(s) or (counter-)transference (see Chapter 8) which may get in the way of pure listening.

The coaching contract

After the first conversation, coach and coachee usually conclude a contract. In the case of internal coaching, it is usually sufficient to make (verbal) agreements concerning:

- the objectives of the coaching
- the topics to be addressed by the coaching, including the way in which you are to work on specific topics, in relation to working on underlying patterns and career or management development issues
- the approach and methods to be used
- the intended effects of the coaching in the workplace
- the method of checking or evaluating whether the objectives and intended results have been achieved

- the length, frequency and duration of the coaching sessions
- the venue for the sessions
- unconditional confidentiality
- reference to an applicable Code of Conduct and conditions (see also Chapter 15).

In the case of external coaching, the usually formal, written contract covers all of the above plus an agreement of the fee, specifying:

- the level of the fee
- any reimbursement of other costs
- the method of payment
- financial arrangements for cancelled sessions.

Summary: structuring the coaching journey

The coaching process involves the following steps:

1. Intake and establishment of a coaching contract.
2. Building and maintaining the relationship.
3. Raising awareness.
4. Refining the contract.
5. Facilitating change.
6. Integration, review and evaluation.
7. Closure.

Preparation by the coach:

- 'empty your mind'
- be aware of how you are feeling at this moment
- decide whether or not you intend to take notes.

Setting for the conversations:

- comfortable chairs set at a wide angle to each other
- moveable table
- tidy, well-lit, pleasant room.

During conversations:

- asking questions
- listening, to the coachee's body language as well as their statements
- mirroring, including the coachee's feelings
- maintaining awareness of yourself as coach.

Ingredients of the coaching contract:

- the objectives and topics of the coaching
- the intended outcomes of the coaching in the workplace
- the method of checking or evaluating intended objectives and outcomes
- the length of each session; the number of sessions and the interval between them
- the venue for the sessions
- unconditional confidentiality
- the level of any fee and reimbursement of other costs.

4
Entering into and ending the coaching relationship

Coach and issue often enter into an interesting interaction with each other. This often begins right at the start of coaching: for example, if the coachee presents an issue *and* an opinion on it, or an interpretation of it. Issue and issue holder become entangled and one wonders where to begin in a coaching conversation – with the issue, with the relationship between coachee and issue, or with the coachee? Just as issue and issue holder in coaching often enter into these patterns and play out recurring 'scripts', the coachee often plays fascinating games with his or her coach – games which are normally related to the initial issue(s) and to the subject matter of the coaching. For the coach, the dynamic of the coaching relationship may give clues to the relationship between the coachee and others and to the relationship between the coachee and his/her issues. For the coachee, the coaching relationship may develop into something meaningful – into a significant relationship which frequently springs to mind even outside the coaching conversations. More than enough reason to enter into, develop and wind down the coaching relationship as carefully as possible, and to take regular time out to consider the nature of the evolving relationship. In addition, minor frustrations in this relationship can have significant consequences for the results of the coaching. For a consideration of really difficult relationships between coach and coachee, and how to interpret and handle them, see Chapter 9.

Entering into a coaching relationship as a theme of coaching

The first impressions that people gain of each other have a significant impact on the course of their subsequent communication. First impressions can, after all, be strong and persistent. They can tell you a lot about the underlying themes, but can also be deceptive. A particularly positive or negative first impression often indicates that something is going on that might obstruct an open, exploratory approach. It is worthwhile registering a number of things consciously right at the outset, such as:

- Are both parties on time, or does one arrive early or late?
- Do they shake hands? What does it feel like? Do they look at each other?
- What associations does this person have for you? Who does (s)he remind you of?
- How do the two parties get on? What body language do you notice?
- Do you use first names? Do you break the ice, or give a formal introduction?

There is no one correct answer to these questions, but it is important to consider them because experience shows that 'minor' impressions at the start can have major consequences later on.

The start of a coaching relationship is often dominated by the needs of both coachee and coach, and on their degree of openness about those needs. The coachee often needs help, and it is quite possible that (s)he may also have a clear need for a specific type of help and a specific approach from the coach. In a sense, such a coachee supplies the problem and the solution right at the outset! The coach needs a coachee in order to be a coach – he or she often has a need to be helpful to someone and to consolidate that helpfulness.

It helps to be aware of the existence of such needs, their translation into specific wishes or their concealment using diversionary tactics, right from the start. Managing them explicitly and in a productive way can then commence, if necessary, right at the start of the coaching relationship.

An example

One of us receives a call from the executive secretary of a large company. She says that one of the directors wants to make an appointment for a coaching conversation. Strikingly, he doesn't call himself but has his secretary make contact. It is also striking that the coachee won't come to the coach: the coaching has to take place in his office.

When it comes to it, the coach is welcomed by the secretary and has to wait a while until the coachee is available – a revealing start, with hindsight! The coachee finds it difficult to make contact. He comes across as somewhat single-minded and pays little heed to the interaction between the people in his department. He finds people difficult, in fact, and looks for ways to avoid people if he doesn't get on with them, instead of discussing the issues openly with them. He feels threatened easily and comes across as anxious. In the first conversation he says that he wants to learn from coaching how to exercise influence better in different contexts. He adds that he wants to come across more forcefully. The coach tells him how he has come across to her, and what influence he has had on her so far, and asks whether there are similarities with the behavioural patterns between him and his colleagues. This generates understanding. Later, the coachee experiments cautiously with different behaviour, paying more attention to interpersonal processes and making them the subject of conversation.

After a hesitant beginning, things gradually get better. He feels more influential and more valued by his colleagues, but still finds it difficult to make contact. Suddenly, the coach is informed that the coaching is over! Saying goodbye, as a form of contact, is also difficult for this coachee. He could have been better prepared for that by the coach.

It is advisable for you, as the coach, to enter into and build up the relationship as consciously as possible. To that end, it may be useful to investigate for yourself – patiently and almost a little suspiciously – how the coachee arrived at his or her issue, and what role you are seen to play in handling the issue and therefore in the life of the coachee. The following thought experiment may be useful in this connection:

- 'What does this coachee actually want? Does (s)he want to get away from something, or to achieve something? To explore something, or to arm themselves against something ...?'
- 'How has the coachee arrived at the situation in which (s)he is recounting their issue? What else might this issue relate to? What does it point to? What might be hidden behind the issue? What is the history of the issue and what attempts have already been made to address it ...?'
- 'Why coaching? What has led to this request? What does (s)he expect from it? What recommendations does (s)he generally accept, and from whom ...?'
- 'And why me? What expectations does this coachee have of me – what prejudices, perhaps – what assumptions about my method? What is the coachee hoping for ...?'
- 'What feelings does this coachee prompt in me? Do I think we get on? What do I think of the quality of our contact? What is (s)he appealing to in me? Can I and do I want to offer it? What is my own interest? And what am I hoping for myself ...?'
- 'What approach is the coachee requesting? What approach do I think myself is best? Coaching or no coaching? Person-focused or problem-focused? Solution-focused or insight-focused? Does the coachee have sufficient strength to handle my preferred approach ...?'
- 'What does this mean for our relationship? How is it going to develop? How am I to enter into that relationship itself? How can I show in my behaviour what kind of relationship I envisage? How can I adopt this coaching approach from my very first meeting ...?'

Once the coaching has started, many types of coach/coachee relationship can develop, often geared very specifically to the specific interaction between this particular coach and this particular coachee. Technically, we refer to *positive transference* or *working alliance*[1] – in other words, to replicating previous helpful relationships in someone's life, making use of the coachee's previous

1.   These terms come from Freud (*inter alia* 1912b), who also provides other useful

experience of other helpful conversations. The following typical forms of positive transference can be differentiated:

- The *guild master/freeman relationship*, in which the coachee presents practical issues and the coach immerses him- or herself in those issues and says something meaningful about them. This relationship is often seen between mentor and mentee, or in supervision.
- The *doctor/patient relationship*, in which the coachee turns him- or herself inside out, revealing uncertainties and emotions as completely as possible; the coach interprets the problems and outlines possible solutions. This relationship often arises with more emotional themes and issues.
- The *midwife/mother relationship*,[2] in which the coach anticipates the coachee's problems and seeks to help provide strength to tackle them. This relationship is characteristic of a very concerned and caring coach.
- The *peer review relationship*, in which coach and coachee look together at the coachee's day-to-day practice and subject it to as independent an examination as possible. They 'dot the i's' together and take a critical look at the coachee's approach and proposals. This relationship often arises in a more insight-focused setting.
- The *old boys relationship*, in which the coachee seeks out the coach as a sparring partner in order to exchange experiences and try out ideas. The coachee often rehearses certain approaches and conversations with the coach. This relationship often arises in the coaching of senior managers.

Of course, in our day-to-day practice we see various mixtures of these typical relationships and we often see a coaching relationship evolve from one to another, depending on changes in the nature of the themes.

Take care that coaching relationships do not deteriorate unnoticed into 'ordinary' significant relationships, like that of a courting couple, rival scientists, a rich uncle and favourite nephew, or a parent and dependent child. The coaching relationship comes into everyone's life after many other important relationships have already been entered into. Almost inevitably, the coaching relationship comes to resemble one or more of its predecessors. This is not a problem in itself, as long as

- it does not happen completely unnoticed, and
- it does not undermine the essence of the coaching relationship (as helping, delineated and for the benefit of the coachee).

phrases such as *zärtliche Übertragung* (tender transference) and *erwartungsvoll bereitgehaltene Libidobesetzung* (expectantly maintained libidinal cathexis).
2. This is the relationship that Socrates entered into with ambitious young men in ancient Athens – see, for example, Plato's *Theaetetus*. However, Socrates combined this welcoming and caring role with that of the 'gadfly' that saw through any gratuitous stories and excuses.

Figure 4.1 Coaching relationships already exist within most households; the
coachee is therefore prepared very early for working alliances of
the kind necessary for coaching

This is also considered in our discussion of transference and counter-transference in Chapter 8. As long as the coach continues to reflect – patiently and
almost suspiciously! – on the nature of the relationship and is not led astray
into non-coaching interventions, any resemblance to other, earlier relationships can only be enriching and instructive. Forces that exert an influence in
all other relationships, such as the quest for inclusion, control, or affection
(see Schutz, 1958 and *Learning with Colleagues*, Chapter 12), will unavoid-
ably also come into play in this coaching relationship. What those forces are,
and how and when they surface, often depends on the coachee's issue and
how the coachee deals with it personally. Following on from this, it is worth
viewing the nature of the evolving relationship (implicitly and explicitly) as
a theme of the coaching itself.

Saying goodbye as a theme of coaching

Most coaching literature does not devote much attention to the end of a coaching journey, yet the end of coaching is certainly an important moment and an
important theme it its own right. In the following paragraphs we examine this
theme, the actual 'goodbye' and the evaluation of a coaching journey.

The psychoanalytic literature, compared with that on coaching, devotes more attention to termination, parting and loss. Growing up always entails saying goodbye: to breastfeeding, nappies, primary school, the parental home, and parents themselves. The process can be a difficult one and ambivalent feelings come into play each time we say goodbye. Saying goodbye is something we have to do throughout our lives and it can sometimes be very traumatic. Saying goodbye within significant relationships is a particularly painful process.

Malan (1995) mentions a number of quite different responses by clients to endings – which can always be related to the main issues in the coaching process:

- Simple gratitude, or a last session very similar to the others – which is the more likely to occur the shorter the coaching.
- A sense of having received 'enough', even though the coach may have misgivings and feel there is more to work on.
- The so-called 'flight into health', where the coachee suddenly has no more issues and says (s)he has resolved them all. This can only be 'apparent health', and may be a way to end the coaching before the coach can announce the ending him/herself.
- Premature withdrawal, where the coachee comes to the penultimate session fully intending to come again and then suddenly decides not to attend the last session. This often represents a way of avoiding feelings about the ending itself (see the example on pages 37–8).
- Intense grief and anger, which seems much more serious that the limited scope of the coaching relationship would indicate. This is a 'transference phenomenon' (see Chapter 8); like the previous response it usually stems from earlier difficult endings in the coachee's life experience when 'normal mourning' was not possible.

Every coaching process has boundaries. As a coach, you want to handle this boundedness professionally. Be aware that saying goodbye can be difficult for your coachee, and try not to add a new negative experience to other painful experiences of saying goodbye. It should not be a simple repetition of old pain – saying goodbye must be made manageable by the departing coachee personally. Ideally, therefore, the coachee herself should say goodbye to the coach and not feel abandoned or rejected. If you are aware that saying goodbye is a relevant theme for the coachee, it is important to facilitate it carefully.

A number of points may help make it easier to say goodbye:

- Make clear arrangements in advance about saying goodbye, so the coachee knows what will happen.
- Bring up the subject of what saying goodbye means to the coachee, if you notice that (s)he finds it difficult to stay or to go away.

- Ask specifically what it means to the coachee to say goodbye to this particular coach, to yourself.
- Be aware that saying goodbye involves a sort of 'mourning process' which can be broken down into phases: denial, anger, depression, acceptance and renewed forward impetus ...
- Think about what saying goodbye means to you: what are you losing, and what holds you back from letting a coachee go?

The actual goodbye

And then it is over: the end of the journey. To be able to round off a coaching relationship well, it is advisable to arrange a final meeting in which you and the coachee can discuss the working relationship, and its meaning to the coachee and his or her future development.

Some coaches ask their coachee to describe their process of development in pictures, in a drawing. Others ask for a reflective report or a learning log. Still others request a verbal conversation. Whatever the case, it is useful to take a look back together to the start of the coaching journey, its stages of development, its outcome and the coachee's future perspectives.

The evaluation of the coaching journey

Saying goodbye is not the same as evaluating a coaching process. By evaluating the coaching after a period of time, the coach confronts the coachee with where (s)he is at that time and the coach learns more about his or her own coaching style. It also allows the coach to demonstrate reflection on his or her own practice and explore opportunities for development. Questions which might be asked in this context include the following:

About the coachee:

- How does the coachee look back on the process and the outcome of the coaching?
- What became of the original objectives?
- What plans did the coachee make at the end of the journey?
- What became of those plans in the intervening period? What new plans, if any, has (s)he made?
- How does the coachee intend to continue the personal process of professional development?

About the coach:

- What has the coach contributed to the coachee's learning process?
- What is the evidence for that contribution?
- How did the coachee experience the interaction during the conversations?

- What were difficult moments in the coaching, and how did the coach handle them?
- What tips does the coachee have for the coach in his or her continued development?

We ourselves experience more and more clearly feelings of loss, or even pain, at saying goodbye at the end of every coaching conversation. This too feels like a break in the relationship and the start of a period in which the coachee is alone again. As a result, we are increasingly moving towards a brief review and evaluation at the end of each conversation, reviewing what went well in this conversation and what less so. A few minutes' evaluation at the end of each coaching conversation helps to facilitate the coachee's transition to the 'world outside'.

It has also proved to be a good idea for the coaching contract to incorporate a formal evaluation and possible refining of the contract halfway through the coaching, especially when other parties such as the coachee's manager were closely involved in setting the objectives for the coaching. The coachee can then go back to these other parties and check if they think the coaching is on track and whether they already experience something changing.

Summary: entering into and ending the coaching relationship

The coaching relationship itself is always a theme of coaching, because:

- the coachee's issues overlap with the way in which the coachee handles them
- the way in which the coachee handles the issues overlaps with how the coachee handles him/herself and others
- the way in which the coachee handles others overlaps with how the coachee handles the coach.

When entering into a coaching relationship, the following factors are crucial:

- the first impression that coach and coachee make on each other
- the different needs that coach and coachee have on entering into the relationship
- the expectations and assumptions that coach and coachee have about each other
- the initial skirmishes which mark the entrance into a coaching relationship of a specific type.

Later on, the coaching relationship often evolves into a significant relationship for the coachee which is reminiscent of, for example:

- a guild master/freeman relationship
- a doctor/patient relationship
- a midwife/mother relationship
- a peer review relationship
- an 'old boys' relationship.

Allowing a helping coaching relationship to deteriorate unnoticed into an ordinary, more two-sided relationship is extremely risky.

Saying goodbye itself is another theme of coaching, and is a painful process that needs to be facilitated and made explicit. It is helpful to spend some time evaluating the coaching, considering factors such as:

- the process and outcome of the coaching
- the coachee's learning process
- the interaction during conversations and the 'difficult moments'
- how the coachee can develop further in relation to his or her issues
- how the coach can develop further as a coach.

Part II

Approaches to coaching

Introduction: 'Authenticity'

Having built a picture of the characteristics and set-up of 'helping conversations' in the first part of this book we intend, in Part II, to outline different approaches taken by the coach in such conversations. This can only be done in a rather abstract and general way that fails to take account of some of the subtlety of coaching conversations. Haven't we seen earlier that coach and coachee exchange information at different levels simultaneously, and that such interwoven and interconnected patterns of information exchange can qualify and even contradict each other? How can we then make unambiguous statements about the approach taken by the coach? Only if the coach is consistent over time and also consistent in all of the various layers of communication? If so, then that is by no means always the case – which is why ironic and paradoxical descriptions, introduced later in Part II (in Chapter 9), are perhaps the most realistic ones.

In order to be able to comment on different coaching approaches, this part of the book assumes for the sake of convenience that the coach is sufficiently consistent:

- across different communication channels, i.e. in his or her own expressive and appellant communication, and in verbal and non-verbal communication, and
- over time; in other words, during all events taking place in longer sections of coaching conversations.

Certainly an inconsistent coach can make things unnecessarily difficult for the coachee, so these assumptions will carry a positive connotation for most readers in most situations.

In the next seven chapters we give a wide-ranging overview of coaching approaches. The different approaches are justified on the basis of our 'window onto the coach' (Chapter 2), and of the historical development of psychotherapy. Coaching may have grown out of management training and sports coaching, but we believe it has a sound foundation in principles and methods of psycho-therapy.[1] We have therefore decided to place it within the context of the main currents of psychotherapy. We realise that, in so doing:

- Implicitly we are making great demands on coaches, demands to which we return in the chapter on the capabilities of the coach (Chapter 12).
- We cannot be exhaustive and will stick to the major trends. Some impor-tant contributions to the coaching profession, such as those that have come out of therapeutic schools like RET, NLP, TA and Gestalt, will not be covered in this book. This is partly because these approaches overlap signif-icantly with approaches that we do introduce. It is also because some of these approaches do not fit into our definition of coaching (see Chapter 1), in which the coach facilitates the coachee's development and so leaves the giving of expert advice to the coachee him- or herself. On the basis of that definition, advice from the coach should serve primarily to stimulate the learning process, with less emphasis on telling the coachee what to do.

In Chapter 12, the approaches introduced in Part II are made more explicit by linking specific interventions – in other words, specific behaviour – to different coaching styles and approaches.

Our own position with respect to the different approaches is largely neutral and eclectic: it is as independent as possible and chooses what is most helpful or effective in a given situation. All of the methods given here, as in *Learning with Colleagues*, can be applied to every coaching issue in principle, although each method does of course have its own specific merits, drawbacks and preferred applications (see Chapter 11). We both have our own personal pref-erences as well, but we are aware that they are not set in stone, and vary with the coachees that we meet and the developmental process that we ourselves undergo. In addition, we believe emphatically that coaches and coachees must discover for themselves which approaches suit them best. Such discoveries are among the most important outcomes of coaching, and we would not wish to deprive anyone of them by stating our own preferences.

In our view, the most important contribution that the coach can make to 'helping conversations' is genuineness – in other words, an honest and authentic interest in the coachee and his or her issues. We believe that spontaneous and genuine interest cannot be replaced by any form of train-ing, study or supervision. In that respect, there is nothing to beat a unique, personal style of coaching.[2] We appreciate that trying out and practising

1. We recommend the book by Bruce Peltier (2001), which provides a more detailed theoretical foundation for coaching in both psychotherapeutical and sports coaching literature.
2. Research has shown that even leading therapists such as Freud, Rogers and Erick-son, in the approaches they described, introduced many methods and techniques which fitted in with their own personalities (Corsini and Wedding, 1989).

new approaches can adversely affect that 'genuineness' in the short term. In the long term, however, we are confident that the genuine interest that a coach can demonstrate is only reinforced and broadened through increasing familiarity with, and study of, different approaches. We believe that another characteristic of genuineness, and hence of good coaches, is that they maintain close links between theory and application – in other words, they are who they claim to be and are happy to be held accountable for the way in which they work. We hope that this part of the book can help coaches to increase the genuineness of their approach.

Part II of the book is structured as follows. After a short historical summary, Chapters 6, 7, 8 and 9 describe four different coaching approaches. In Chapter 10 all four are translated into specific methods, as far as this is possible, in the form of consecutive steps in coaching conversations. In Chapter 11 we examine the applicability of the different approaches and methods and give suggestions arising from both research results and experience.

This structure is intended to give coaches the opportunity:

- to reflect on their own approach to coaching conversations and to pick up new ideas
- to increase their flexibility by considering a range of approaches and by investigating when to apply which approach
- to bring their genuineness more to the fore by harmonising reflection and action or theory and practice as far as possible
- to gain inspiration for (even) more authentic coaching, rather than to learn recipes for 'good' coaching.

5
Historic roots and summary of approaches

Personal development through coaching may have grown out of management training and sports coaching but it has much in common, in our view, with the older field of psychotherapy (see also Peltier, 2001). As a consequence, we look primarily to psychotherapy to find historic roots for various coaching approaches. In the history of psychotherapy different authors have made different choices and different recommendations, often related to their own approach or personality, or to the type of clients for whom their approach was developed. Strangely, research has shown that there is much more agreement between psychotherapists in practice than there is in theory (Corsini and Wedding, 1989). Therapists using completely different theoretical approaches therefore do largely the same things in the consulting room.

It is interesting to review the main currents of psychotherapy one by one, because the evaluations made by psychotherapists are also relevant to the choices you can make as a coach. We therefore propose a 'selectively eclectic' approach to coaching, where the coach considers various options and chooses the one that fits best in the given situation and with their own personality and expertise as a coach.

Historic roots

Table 5.1 offers a brief summary. In order to organise the different psychotherapeutic approaches, we consider how a number of important currents in psychotherapy handle the therapist's involvement in the client's learning objectives. In all psychotherapy, and also in coaching, the therapist/coach becomes part of the client's past and risks doing things that consolidate, instead of changing, problematic aspects from that past. This can happen, for example, if the coach only goes through the motions, or attempts to change from the outside things that can only be changed from the inside by the coachee.

An extremely clear-cut formulation of this basic dilemma within psychotherapy or coaching can be found in the book *Strategies of*

Psychotherapy (Haley, 1963), where Haley asserts that clients generally seek out psychotherapy as a last resort in order *not* to change, in order to stay the same despite external pressure. What they then ask of the therapist is paradoxical: 'Change me without changing me!' This poses a dilemma for the therapist, who is being asked to intervene, on the one hand, but on the other hand to leave the client the same! Different currents handle this basic dilemma differently, as we see in the Table 5.1.

Each of these four main currents in psychotherapy has influenced the way in which professionals in organisations are coached. Each current has a different emphasis, which can be useful at different times and with different coachees. In the following chapters we show how these different approaches found their way into our own coaching practice. We introduce four approaches that follow on from these four main currents:

- *Directive coaching:* attempting to improve from the outside.
- *Person-centred coaching:* attempting to move the focus inside.
- *Analytic coaching:* attempting to understand from the inside.
- *Paradoxical coaching:* attempting to upset, surprise or manipulate from the outside.

Table 5.1 The main currents of psychotherapy and their approach to the dilemma

	Some leading figures	Emphasis is on	How to handle the 'basic dilemma'
Analytic/ Psychodynamic	Sigmund Freud Carl Jung Melanie Klein	Primary process thinking Conflicts Transference Understanding and interpretation	Deferment, until: Emergence of the dilemma in this interaction
Cognitive/ Behavioural	Ivan Pavlov Albert Ellis Burrhus Skinner Aaron Beck	Rational analysis Step-by-step plan	Counter-question Finding solutions
Person-centred/ Humanistic	Carl Rogers Abraham Maslow	Internal (self-) evaluation Self-actualisation	Complete acceptance Relaxed
Paradoxical/ Provocative	Milton Erickson Gregory Bateson Jay Haley Frank Farrelly	Paradoxes Drawing on and mobilising defences	Posing a 'counter-paradox' Positive reinforcement

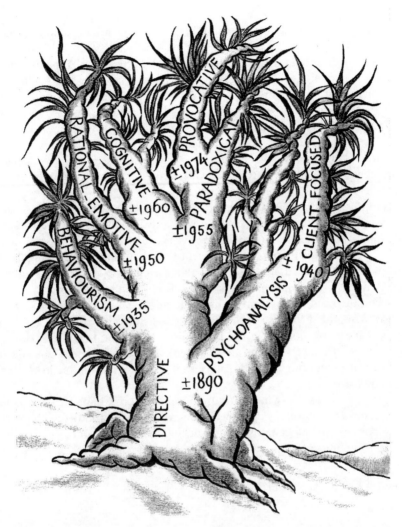

Figure 5.1. A 'family tree' illustrating the growth of different therapeutic trends

1890: The directive trunk splits into two, with the advent of psychoanalysis.

1935: The directive trunk sprouts a new branch – behaviourism.

1940: A branch splits off from the psychoanalytic trunk – client-focused or Rogerian counselling.

1950: The directive trunk sprouts a new branch – the rational-emotive approach.

1955: The directive trunk sprouts a new branch – the paradoxical approach, and (in 1974) the provocative approach.

1960: The directive trunk sprouts a new branch – the cognitive approach.

Roots in the personality of the coach

Depending on his or her own personality, every coach has personal preferences which make certain approaches more attractive than others. It is a good idea to fill in your own coaching profile at this point (Appendix A) so that you can compare your own approach with the four approaches discussed here. But please note – if you do not ask your coachees or colleagues to fill in Appendix A as well, this will only be a self-report. Self-reports are of limited value because you are reporting only what you think about yourself, not what you actually do as a coach.

Table 5.2 illustrates the preferences that characterise four different approaches to coaching, within five different polarities. 'L' stands for the 'left-hand pole' and 'R' for the 'right-hand pole'.

The different approaches can also be placed in the 'window on the coach' matrix in Chapter 2. Under the horizontal axis, 'analytic' and 'person-centred' appear next to each other while above the horizontal axis are the 'directive' and 'paradoxical' approaches, except that they come out at roughly the same place. One special directive approach (see Chapter 6) is the only one to appear in the first quadrant – this is 'solution-focused' coaching, which is strongly influenced by solution-focused therapy.

Otherwise, the directive coaching approaches introduced in this book are less directive than most therapies in the behavioural and cognitive domain (see Hawton et al., 1989). The coachee generally submits less to the coach's authority, although this may take place to a greater extent in mentoring and 'coaching leadership'.

Figure 5.2 shows the 'window onto the coach' from Chapter 2 once again, with a number of different approaches described in the following chapters.

For more specific suggestions about coaching styles, interventions and conversational techniques appropriate to each of these approaches, see Chapter 12.

Table 5.2 Preferred approaches in different coaching methods

	Directive coaching	Person-centred coaching	Analytic coaching	Paradoxical coaching
Directive ⟷ Non-directive	L	R	R	L
Analytic ⟷ Intuitive	–	R	L	L
Oriented towards the future ⟷ Oriented towards the present	L	R	R	L
Solution-focused ⟷ Development-focused	L	R	–	L
Focused on change ⟷ Accepting	L	R	R	L

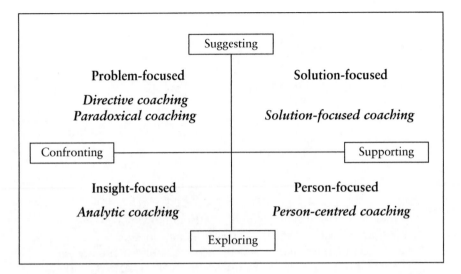

Figure 5.2 The window onto the coach with specific approaches

Summary: historic roots and summary of approaches

Our summary is based on the following four main currents in psychotherapy:

- analytic or psychodynamic therapies
- cognitive or behavioural therapies
- person-centred or Rogerian therapies
- paradoxical, ironic or provocative therapies.

Based on this distinction, and on different approaches developed in part by psychotherapists, we arrive at the following specific approaches:

- Directive coaching: attempting to improve from the outside, such as:
  - the GROW method
  - the solution-focused method.
- Person-centred coaching: attempting to move the focus inside.
- Analytic coaching: attempting to understand from the inside, such as:
  - the analytic and organisation coach method
  - the ladder method.
- Paradoxical coaching: attempting to upset, surprise or manipulate from the outside, such as
  - the ironic method
  - the paradoxical method
  - the provocative method.

6
Directive coaching:
Structuring with an objective

Your every separate action should contribute towards an integrated life; and if each of them, so far as it can, does its part to this end, be satisfied; for that is something which nobody can prevent. 'There will be interferences from without,' you say? Even so, they will not affect the justice, prudence, and reasonableness of your intentions. 'No, but some kind of practical action may be prevented.' Perhaps; yet if you submit to the frustration with a good grace, and are sensible enough to accept what offers itself instead, you can substitute some alternative course which will be equally consistent with the integration we are speaking of.

Marcus Aurelius, *Meditations*

Introduction: the coach at the helm

The most basic and straightforward coaching approach is undoubtedly the *directive* approach, in which the coach keeps a grip on the conversations and puts the coachee on a leash, so to speak, providing encouragement and helping him or her resolve their issues.[1] This book does not describe the most directive methods, which simply involve the coach answering the coachee's questions and explaining how to tackle the issues arising. These sorts of directive technique are not examined more closely because we believe that coaching always focuses on helping the coachee to find his or her own

---

1. In fact, the directive approach has the longest history of all, because an age-old tradition of restraint, disciplining conversations and hypnosis of psychiatric patients is entirely in keeping with this approach. For an introduction to the field of modern directive therapeutic techniques, see Hawton et al. (1989). Otherwise, the description 'cognitive and behavioural' is a more common description, at least in psychotherapy, than 'directive'. This also highlights the distinction with the systemic and paradoxical approaches (see Chapter 9), which are also directive. We retain the word 'directive', nevertheless, because it appears more frequently in the coaching literature.

answers (see also the definitions in Chapter 1). We do discuss a number of extreme directive methods in Chapter 9, in which the coachee does receive answers to his or her questions, albeit highly absurd ones. These are given with a completely different aim in mind than that of providing a solution – namely, that of mobilising the coachee's own problem-solving abilities.

This chapter outlines two methods in which the coach is purely *directive* in the structuring of the conversation, but purely *facilitating* with respect to the content of the issue: the GROW method and the 'solution-focused' method. Both methods are directive with regard to the conversation itself but open or 'empty' with regard to the content of the conversation. These coaching methods can be used for any subject matter.

> *An example*
> The coachee has become bogged down in his job. He experiences himself as being controlled by the issues of the day while he feels a need to exert more control himself. He has become stressed and his employer has terminated his temporary contract. He has time to think about what he expects from a new job. He wants to learn how to avoid the same pitfalls and how to exercise more control in the future. His therapist refers him to a coach. They agree on a course of action: the coach will facilitate his search for a new job, where he hopes to adopt a different attitude.
>
> In the subsequent conversations, and in the coachee's homework between sessions, they explore the sources of his energy (using an energy diary), how he has made decisions in his life so far (using a biography assignment), what he is looking for in a job (using a 'career drivers' questionnaire) and what his main qualities are. He starts his job hunt (via the Internet, newspapers, his own network and the coach's contacts) and is invited to attend a number of interviews. He rehearses the final interview with his coach and is offered the job.

Goal-oriented coaching: the GROW method

A coaching method which has been very successful in organisational settings is John Whitmore's GROW method (1992). The origins of the method betray the roots of 'coaching' in sports coaching: Whitmore based his book on *The Inner Game of Tennis* by the tennis coach Gallwey (1974). Thanks to its rigid structure and ease of use, with its pre-prepared questions, this form of coaching can be quickly learned and applied in a wide variety of situations. Even ten-minute informal coaching conversations can be fitted into the GROW format.

The structure of a GROW coaching conversation is an easily remembered acronym:

1. *G for Goal:* ask about the coachee's goal or objective, as far as the issue is concerned and as far as this conversation is concerned.
2. *R for Reality:* ask for a description of the reality relevant to this issue.
3. *O for Options:* ask about the different options open to the coachee.
4. *W for Will:* ask about the coachee's decision and the strength of his or her accompanying willpower.

In the following paragraphs we go through the different stages of the coaching conversation according to Whitmore (1992), step by step.

Step 1: the personal goal

The coach starts by asking the coachee about the goal of this conversation, even before coach and coachee explore the background and context. This helps the coachee to focus on the future and, right at the start of the coaching conversation, to state the direction (s)he wants the coaching session to take, as well as his or her ultimate personal goal. This goal may be adjusted after Step 2, the reality test.

The coach can ask about both potential goals: the goal for this session and the goal as far as the problem or issue is concerned. If the latter, the 'ultimate goal', also depends on external circumstances outside the coachee's control, the coach also asks about a 'personal target': what does the coachee hope to achieve personally en route to the envisaged ultimate goal.

The coach is looking for a positive formulation of the goal and checks that it is specific, measurable, attainable, relevant and time-bound (these are known as the 'SMART' characteristics).

Sample questions relating to G: the goal:

*   What is the goal of this conversation?
*   What exactly do you want to achieve - in the short term and in the long term?
*   Is this an ultimate goal or a target?
*   If it is an ultimate goal, what is the associated target?
*   When do you want to have achieved it?
*   To what extent is it positive – in other words, a challenge, attainable, measurable?
*   What intermediate steps are involved, and which milestones?
*   In how much detail do you expect to be able to work on this in this session?

Step 2: the underlying reality

The coach attempts to elicit an objective description of the coachee's reality. The coachee is asked to describe, as objectively as possible, how things stand at the moment with regard both to achieving the goal and other relevant factors.

The intention is to gather as much factual and measurable information as possible about the context and background. In the face of value judgments, personal biases and indirectly expressed emotions, the coach perseveres with targeted open questions. Questions focusing on matters of fact, such as 'what', 'who', 'when' and 'how much', are more useful in this respect than questions that elicit opinions and rationalisations, such as 'why' and, to a lesser extent, 'how'.

The coach is looking for facts and circumstances, specific actions taken, obstacles standing in the way of fulfilment and specific sources which can be drawn on, in terms of time, money and manpower for example.

Sample questions relating to R: the reality:

- What is happening now? (What? Where? When? How much?)
- What is the situation exactly?
- Who are the parties involved?
- What exactly is the crux or essence of the problem?
- What exactly are you concerned about in relation to the current situation?
- What have you done about it so far, and with what results?
- What prevented you from doing more?
- How much control do you yourself have over the situation?
- Who else has control, and to what extent?
- What are the main obstacles in your path?
- What internal obstacles still exist?
- What sources can you tap into in order to overcome those obstacles?
- What other resources do you need? How can you get them?
- How does it feel exactly? What emotion is that? What effect does that emotion have on you?
- How would you rate your own confidence on a scale from 1 to 10?
- What exactly are you afraid of?
- What circumstances are reinforcing your self-confidence at this moment?

Step 3: the possible alternatives
The coach helps the coachee maximise his or her own freedom of choice, by asking for possible alternatives. The intention is to gather together as many options as possible, so once the coachee has made an exhaustive list, the coach generally asks for 'just one more'. All conceivable (and also inconceivable) options are welcome – the more the better.

The coach is looking for positive options, possibilities and alternatives. As soon as the coachee comes up with restrictions or reservations about certain options the coach asks: 'What would the option be like if those restrictions or reservations weren't there?' ('What if ...?'). The coach is hesitant to contribute personal suggestions because that would make him or her an expert advisor. Options provided by the coach may prompt resistance, or receive a disproportionately high rating in the coachee's estimation. The coach does not make any suggestions without checking that they are really welcome, and ensuring the coachee has already made a complete personal list.

Sample questions relating to O: the options:

- What are all the different ways in which you could approach this issue?
- What options do you have?
- Make a list of different alternatives, important and less important, complete and partial solutions.
- What else could you do?
- What would you do if you had more time, or a bigger budget, or if you were the boss?
- What would you do if you could start all over again?
- What would you do if all circumstances were under your control?
- Would you perhaps like to hear a suggestion from me?
- What are the pros and cons of all of these different possibilities?
- Which option would produce the best result?
- Which option appeals to you most or feels best?
- Which would give you the most satisfaction?
- Would it be convenient to combine options?

Step 4: determining commitment

The coach attempts to round off the conversation with a sound decision by the coachee – or, if necessary, with the conclusion that the original goal was too ambitious and no decision can be taken. The coach helps the coachee to decide what to do and when – and how likely it is that (s)he will actually act on that decision. It is important for the coach to remain outside the decision-making process. There is a real risk that the coachee will take a 'decision' now only for form's sake or for the sake of the coach, which would of course be a decision of no actual value.

The coach aims to ask, in turn:

- which alternative or combination of options the coachee chooses;
- when the option is to be put into effect, and with what kind of assistance; and
- how great the coachee's commitment is.

Despite this orientation towards closure, the coachee should not feel rushed. If this is the case, it usually comes from a desire on the part of the coach, overtly or covertly, to push the coachee towards a specific decision or course of action. It is therefore a good test, at the end of the conversation, to ask to what extent the coachee has felt (s)he had worked on his or her own authority in this conversation.

Sample questions relating to W: the will:

- What are you going to do?
- Which option, or combination of options, are you going to choose?
- When are you going to do that?
- Will that meet your goal?
- Does this conclusion meet your goal for this conversation?
- What obstacles do you expect, and how are you going to overcome them?
- What internal obstacles do you perceive within yourself?
- How are you going to overcome that internal resistance?
- Who needs to know?
- What help do you need and how are you going to get it?
- What can I do for you in order to support you?
- Indicate on a scale from 1 to 10 how likely it is that you will carry out that action.
- If lower than 10: why not 10? What can you do to make it a 10?
- If lower than 8: is it not better to give up? (As it seems unlikely that you will actually do it.)
- Is there anything else we should talk about, or have we finished?

Positive coaching: the solution-focused method

Solution-focused coaching is an approach derived from solution-focused brief psychotherapy.[2] This current in psychotherapy developed as a reaction to many variants of behavioural and cognitive therapy which were invented as 'problem-focused therapies'. In those variants, therapists worked mainly on exploring problems, interrupting and replacing clients' ineffective solutions. The inventors of solution-focused therapy discovered that building on 'exceptional moments' (times when the problem did not

---

2. *Solution-focused* brief psychotherapy was developed at the Brief Family Therapy Center in Milwaukee and at the Institute for the Study of Therapeutic Change in Chicago, by Insoo Kim Berg, Steve de Shazer, Barry Duncan, Scott Miller and others. In management consultancy and coaching there is a very similar approach known as *Appreciative Inquiry* (see Cooperrider and Srivastva, 1987). This chapter borrows from *Keys To Solution In Brief Therapy* by De Shazer (1985) and *Interviewing for Solutions* by De Jong and Berg (2001).

Figure 6.1 Directive, goal-oriented coaching sometimes has a lot of impact

exist or was less serious) had much more effect on their clients. Instead of advising clients to try out different solutions (therapist-centred), they encouraged clients to do more of what already seemed to be helping, or to do more of what they were already doing when the problem did not arise (client-centred). In so doing, they were working towards a form of therapy that had maximum effect in minimum time.

An important difference between solution-focused coaching and the conventional 'psychoanalytic' approach (Chapter 8) is that the latter establishes causal connections between past and present (phenomena emerge from an underlying structure). In the solution-focused approach, causal connections are not taken as the starting point; causes are regarded as 'narrative constructions' (stories) constructed by the coachee him- or herself. There is no absolute truth; on the contrary, we are constantly constructing our own world (Gergen, 1999). We do this by talking about it and by attaching our own meaning or interpretation to it. Language therefore shapes reality. The coach is not an expert, but explores the stories together with the coachee, challenges him or her to find new definitions and to construct a future in which the problem no longer arises. The coach can help by steering the conversation in that particular direction.

Basic principles of solution-focused coaching

The basic principles of this coaching style are:

- Coachees have access to all the resources they need in order to be able to change. Change is inevitable, because stability is an illusion. The coach encourages change by working together with the coachee.
- No problem is ever-present; there are always times when a problem does not present itself. The coach investigates what the coachee is doing differently or how (s)he is thinking differently, at those times.
- The coach can use coachees' fantasies about the future in order to construct achievable solutions.

In this approach, the coach's task is to accept the problem as presented by the coachee. There is therefore no need for an exhaustive diagnosis or problem analysis. It is not necessary to know precisely how problems came about. What is useful is to concentrate on solutions, asking appropriate questions. 'How would your work look then?' 'What would you be thinking?' 'What would you be doing?' 'How would you be feeling?' The art is to listen to the coachee's story without having any theories of your own in mind (because that would mean you pay less attention to the coachee's theories) and to construct new stories about the coachee's life together, starting from the premise that if you don't like your circumstances or your work, at least you can change your stories about it. By making new definitions, the coachee's experience changes and it becomes easier for him or her to start to act differently. Moreover, talking about solutions is a more motivating experience than talking about problems.

Approach

In order to construct a new story, it is best to start at the beginning. A coaching conversation in this style is characterised by questions focusing on what the coachee is good at, on the exceptions to the problem and on the hypothetical solutions (s)he is considering. You challenge the coachee to suggest specifically and in detail how things could be improved. You draw on the coachee's own problem-solving skills. Understanding the problems and their origins is not necessary.

The coach is concerned with keeping a solution-focused conversation going, by:

- emphasising the coachee's abilities and praising his/her inherent strengths;
- asking for examples of situations in which the coachee did not experience the problem (exceptions); and
- asking about behaviours on the part of the coachee that made a positive difference (successes).

The coach disregards elaborate descriptions of the problem as far as possible. This also applies to blame attributed to third parties and solutions which are outside the coachee's control. The coach helps the coachee to set realistic personal objectives. Minor changes now are sufficient to bring about bigger changes later on.

The coachee embarks on a voyage of discovery around everything that (s)he is already doing right, so that the homework is often: 'Go away and do more of the same'. This leads to successful experiences which the coachee can talk about, and as a result, allow the coachee to take charge personally. The coachee is the expert and finds the solutions. The coach helps with support and praise for what has been achieved.

An important question in solution-focused coaching is the 'miracle question', which asks the coachee to imagine exactly how his or her situation will have changed once the problem is solved.

> ### An example of the 'miracle question'
> Imagine that a miracle occurs one night while you're asleep and the problem that you raised here is solved as a result. But you don't know that the miracle has occurred. What will be different at work the next morning? What will show you that the miracle has occurred and that your problems have disappeared?

The answer to this question gives a clear picture of what the coachee wants to change and what (s)he can do personally to achieve that goal. The coach can have the coachee rate the current situation on a scale from 0 (in which the problem is overwhelmingly dominant) to 10 (in which the problem has disappeared). This makes it possible to track small changes.

Each coaching session ends with the coach giving feedback, praising the coachee on progress and providing relevant homework assignments.

Types of questions
A coaching conversation in the solution-focused style follows the structure outlined below, which is derived from current protocols.

In the first conversation:

- *Problem:* 'What brings you here? How is this a problem for you? What have you already tried? What was useful? What helped?'
- *Objective:* 'What do you want to change as a result of the coaching?' ('Miracle question'; further questions about what would be different.)
- *Exceptions:* 'Are there times when the problem does not arise? When, and what happens then? Are there times when the problem is less serious? When, and what happens then?' (Ask for details; praise the coachee on what (s)he did at the time.)

- *Rating:* improvement since request for coaching; motivation; confidence (all on a scale of 1–10).
- *Feedback:* compliments, reason for the homework assignments (from reflection to doing, depending on whether the coachee is seen as *visitor*, *complainer* or *customer* – see below), setting homework.

In the follow-up conversation:

- Ask about improvements: 'What has improved since our last conversation?'
- Details: 'How is it going? How are you doing that? Is that new for you? What is the effect on X?'
- Compliments on behaviour.
- Continue to ask questions: 'And what else is better?'
- Positive suggestion: 'Do more of the same!'
- Rate the progress (scale 1–10).
- Feedback: compliments, reason for homework, homework itself.
- Signing up for another session: 'How much time do you need for that? When do you want to come back?'

Application

Clearly, the solution-focused method does not make any recommendations for an in-depth exploration and analysis of the problems. In some cases it is necessary to find out more about the problem, but only if it cannot be done more simply and in a more solution-focused way. You can continue to persevere with the solution-focused style if:

- an improvement has already occurred between the request for coaching and the first conversation
- there are exceptions to the problem – in other words, occasions where the problem does not arise or is less serious
- a hypothetical solution can be formulated – a description in behavioural terms of what would be different if the problem were resolved completely.

In other words, according to solution-focused coaches, in the vast majority of cases you can work directly towards a solution without first analysing the problem itself in depth.

The solution-focused coaching style works best if the coachee is open to solution-focused suggestions relating to his or her own behaviour. In that respect, together with De Jong and Berg (2001), we distinguish between 'visitors', 'complainers' and 'customers'.

- *Visitors* are coachees who don't think they have a problem. They are often sent by their bosses and just want to be left in peace. Minimal coaching is possible in these cases. The coach can do no more than attempt to create a working relationship in which coaching becomes possible, by recognising the coachee's situation, supporting and praising him or her, and being as 'hospitable' as possible.

- *Complainers* do provide information about their problem, but see themselves neither as part of the problem nor of the solution. In such cases, the coach can encourage the coachee to reflect on the real possibility of personal change.
- *Customers* are the ideal coachees for the solution-focused coach. They say they want to do something about the problem themselves. The coach can give customers homework with some expectation that they will actually do it.

An example

The coachee works in a government department where she feels completely isolated. Like a dedicated professional, she churns out memoranda and reports, only for them to remain unread. What she does is clever, but she's doing it all on her own. She doesn't involve any colleagues because she's afraid they won't really be able to understand what she's doing. Gradually, she starts to feel thoroughly miserable and under a lot of stress. She is not getting enough sleep, all sorts of ideas keep going round in her head, and she is touchy at home. She no longer finds any enjoyment in her hobbies.

Figure 6.2 Solution-focused coaching can put you back on the right track

This is no time for confrontational interventions, as this approach might only cause the coachee to become overly stressed. The coach therefore opts for reinforcing interventions: exploring when the coachee feels better and when things are going well. The coach tries to identify times when the coachee does experience collaboration and satisfaction and, together with the coachee, works out homework assignments which will enable closer collaboration.

These lead to positive experiences. The coachee notices that colleagues are open to her if she acts with greater initiative, and that it is inspiring to think about things together. She becomes more and more enthusiastic and finds that, as time passes, she is better able to make a real contribution. One small step at a time, she goes a long way.

Summary: directive coaching

A characteristic feature of directive coaching approaches is that the coach takes a strong lead, and either structures the conversations or comes up with solutions and hands out assignments.

Two directive methods are introduced:

1. The GROW method

Goal-oriented coaching, oriented towards the future: the coach facilitates the coachee and proposes ways of achieving a stated goal. Conversations are structured as follows:

- G for Goal: have the coachee formulate the outcome or objective personally.
- R for Reality: ask for a description of the reality relevant to this issue.
- O for Options: ask about the various options open to the coachee.
- W for Will: ask about the coachee's decision and commitment.

2. The solution-focused method

Solution-focused coaching, moving away from the problem: the coach tries to find situations when the problem does not arise, looks for reasons for those positive experiences, and attempts to build on them. Conversations are structured as follows:

- *Objective*: What do you want to achieve?
- *Solutions now*: What is going better already? How exactly? What positive exceptions do you experience?
- *Characteristics of solutions*: What tells you that things are going better ('miracle question')?
- *Feedback for solutions*: Positive evaluation and compliments.
- *Reinforcement of solutions*: Reinforcing what is already going well with the aid of homework.

The solution-focused method distinguishes three types of coachee, and can actually help only the third group:

- *Visitors*: don't think they have a problem.
- *Complainers*: don't see themselves as part of their problem.
- *Customers*: indicate that they want to do something about their problem.

7

Person-centred coaching:
Facilitating the coachee

The most personal is the most universal.
Carl Rogers, *On Becoming a Person*

Introduction: counselling as a form of coaching

'Person-centred counselling' is a form of coaching in which the coachee is welcomed entirely on his or her own terms and is given a maximum of space to work in his or her own way on personal issues. The coach refrains as far as possible from any form of direction, contributes a minimum of new information or advice, and acts as a sort of partner and companion in the coachee's process of development. We might start by considering where counselling lies in terms of the various facilitating styles that we can identify (see *Learning with Colleagues*, Chapter 16), namely:

- *Expert:* focused on the coachee's issues and problems.
- *Process manager:* focused on the process between the coachee and his or her problems.
- *Trainer:* focused on the skills and abilities of the coachee.
- *Developer:* focused on the person and values of the coachee.

The counsellor is very much in the camp of the developer. Counselling is therefore a form of coaching in which the coachee is always at the centre; it focuses on increasing the self-confidence, strength and abilities of the coachee personally. In the counselling approach the coachee as a person is central from the outset, and coach and coachee tackle the problems and issues on that basis.

An example
The coachee is silent at the start of the conversation and looks at the coach in a wait-and-see mode. The coach looks back with a friendly smile and full of expectation. The situation starts to resemble a children's game in which players try to out-stare each

other without blinking or looking away. Until the coachee shrugs her shoulders and bursts out slightly provocatively, 'Oh well, I suppose I'll have to do it myself then ... that's what you're trying to tell me, isn't it? I decide what to talk about.'

The coach ignores her own inclinations to, first, give a response, second, start to structure the conversation, and third, interpret the coachee's striking behaviour. Perhaps out of shyness, perhaps because no other specific option presents itself, she keeps smiling in a friendly and inviting way, until the following sentence issues forth: 'What do you want to talk about today? We agreed to look at specific practical issues, but also at your career development. Do you want to start somewhere?'

There is another short silence, until the coachee clears her throat and says: 'You know, I've prepared for this conversation and have already gone through a few things.' The unaccustomed openness, willingness and compliance of the coach at the start of this conversation makes such an impression that the coachee refers to it frequently in subsequent conversations: 'You showed me then that I could really bring anything to these conversations.'

Carl Rogers on counselling

The psychologist Carl Rogers has promoted person-centred counselling in a way that can be inspiring for the coach. Rogers tends towards an extreme position, in which the coach contributes and directs as little as possible. In his view, the coach in the first instance should provide the conditions that enable the coachee to design and undergo a personal process of growth or learning. The coach can do this primarily by offering empathy, respect, warmth and genuineness in his or her relationship with the coachee (Rogers, 1957).

In Rogers' person-centred approach, the following beliefs are central:[1]

- Confidence in the *self-actualisation* of the coachee: Rogers assumes this self-actualisation to be a fundamental, driving force of personality. If all circumstances are favourable and there is nothing to obstruct the personality, it will grow into an 'optimal individual form': an ever-increasing development and refinement of personal capabilities. Rogers therefore has a deep and unshakeable confidence in every personality and in its ability to develop ever-greater balance and health.
- In order to create the favourable conditions referred to above, the coach must accept the coachee unconditionally. Outside the counselling relationship, unconditional acceptance by another person who has no wish to

1. Rogers' ideas about counselling appear in many publications. We particularly recommend *On Becoming A Person* (1961), about individual counselling, and *Carl Rogers On Encounter Groups* (1970), about team counselling.

influence them is relatively rare. Within the counselling relationship, this attitude on the part of the coach is essential for the coachee's development.

- The coachee is the focal point of the counselling. This is made possible by approaching the coachee with as much empathy as possible. By 'empathy', Rogers means the ability to take on board the coachee's perceptions, experiences and concerns as if they were the coach's own. Empathy means identifying your own perspective completely to that of the coachee and also demonstrating the extent to which you have succeeded (however imperfectly) in understanding him or her from the inside, thereby seeking even greater understanding.

- It is asking a lot of the coach to meet the coachee with unconditional acceptance and empathy. According to Rogers, the coach can do this only if (s)he also accepts him- or herself unconditionally and is therefore free of differences between the way (s)he 'is' and the way (s)he 'should be or would like to be' in his or her own eyes. Rogers calls these differences *incongruences*. What is therefore required of the coach is to be congruent. A congruent coach is above all genuine, especially with respect to him- or herself, and so accepts all of the internal feelings – positive and negative – with respect to the coachee. Whether or not all of those feelings are expressed depends on the contribution that this would make towards offering safety and unconditional acceptance. Congruence combined with empathy does call for a great deal of openness on the part of the coach with regard to what is going on in his or her own mind. Rogers called this *transparency*: showing what is going on in yourself in response to issues of the coachee.

Techniques of the counsellor

Structuring techniques

The coach finds diary space for the coachee and draws up a type of contract in which the coachee states learning objectives for the coaching process. The coachee determines the number and frequency of meetings. During the coaching process the coach reflects the coachee's contribution regularly by summarising and referring to links in the material submitted.

Directive techniques

All directive techniques which involve structuring the conversation, making suggestions, or giving feedback, advice, assignments or instructions are quite out of place here. The aim is that the coachee should work on personal issues at his or her own pace and in his or her own way. The only direction from the coach serves to ensure that this comes about – in other words, the initiative in the conversation is left to the coachee. Rogers was well aware that the complete avoidance of directive tendencies is not feasible in practice and

Figure 7.1 The counsellor approaches the coachee with an unconditionally positive regard

is in itself a sort of direction. Using himself as an example, he writes that he is generally interested in emotions and deeper personal convictions, such as standards and values (Rogers, 1961). He is not surprised, therefore, that his own counselling conversations were often concerned with those more personal layers of the communication However, Rogers does go so far as to avoid giving any form of feedback. Feedback, or opinions offered by the coach, which always have an element of appreciation or rejection about them, would be too directive because the viewpoint from which the feedback is given (the 'locus of evaluation' – Raskin, 1952) is an external one. For Rogers, appreciation and rejection act as conditional acceptance of the coachee, and are consequently quite inappropriate.

Non-directive techniques
Counselling makes particular use of techniques involving an accepting presence, a listening, relaxed attitude and a minimum of 'initiating' behaviour. The primary aim here is to observe closely – and 'from the inside', as it were – the words, opinions, behaviours and emotions of the coachee. The coach attempts, so to speak, to look together with the coachee and through the coachee's eyes. Other non-directive interventions are those which communicate safety and acceptance within the counselling relationship, such as a sympathetic smile, eye contact, relaxed movements and gestures that emphasise proximity. The coach says little about him- or herself, usually only in

response to a direct question from the coachee. When the coach does so, (s)he tries to be as genuine and truthful as possible – in accordance with the principle of transparency.

It is important to point out that these techniques for counselling provide a sound basis for any form of coaching. In coaching, coach and coachee consider the coachee's issue together, so it is always important for the coach to observe issues carefully and to understand them from the personal perspective of the coachee. In counselling these observational techniques are in fact the only techniques that are recommended, and any other intervention by the coach, such as direction or analysis, is disruptive to the coachee. The coach adopts a receptive attitude and need not add anything new, original or helpful. Indeed, counselling benefits greatly if the coach can control any selfish inclination to be helpful or inventive.

Approach to counselling

When we see counsellors at work or watch videos featuring Carl Rogers,[2] we can identify a number of non-directive interventions:

- *Invitations* to speak, in complete openness and without pressure to do so in any specific way.
- *Deepening* by attention, summaries and reflecting feelings. Sometimes the coach uses a single, non-directional, open question, but not often. Usually, time and space is given as well as summaries, often almost word-for-word, and reflections of feelings. In addition, some summaries are deepening because they also summarise what can be read between the lines.
- *Reinforcing contact* by encouragement, gestures and words which increase contact, as well as self-disclosure, primarily relating to how the coach is feeling here and now.

In the appendices to this book we provide two instruments which may help you to become more proficient as a counsellor. Appendix C contains a 'sliding scale of push and pull', to demonstrate that you have both directing and facilitating alternatives at any moment in a conversation. In our view, pure 'pulling' behaviour is an extremely valuable skill for a coach (see also Chapter 12, where we summarise the associated interventions in terms of the styles 'exploring' and 'supporting', which we consider to be the most pure coaching styles). Appendix D contains the 'person-centred reflection form', an instrument which enables you to look back at a coaching conversation and identify the many obstacles to a non-directive or person-centred approach to coaching within yourself.

2. See, for example, *Carl Rogers Counsels an Individual on Hurt and Anger*, or *The Right To Be Desperate*, both available from Concord Film, Ipswich.

Summary: person-centred coaching

Counselling is a form of coaching in which:

- The coachee is, as far as possible, at the centre of attention.
- Coach and coachee work from the coachee's perspective and at the coachee's pace.
- The coachee can develop as autonomously as possible.

Basic principles of counselling:

- Self-actualisation of the coachee: the coachee has genuine freedom to develop in the right direction by him/herself.
- Unconditional acceptance and an unconditional positive regard.
- The coach seeks as much personal empathy with the coachee as possible.
- The coach's behaviour is as congruent and as genuine as possible.
- The coach is transparent about his or her own feelings and convictions.

The following basic principles result in a counselling approach that is as non-directive as possible:

- Give the coachee as much space and acceptance as possible.
- Understand the coachee as much as possible on his or her own terms.
- Reinforce contact by encouragement, proximity and self-disclosure.
- Let observation, evaluation and monitoring take place from the coachee's perspective as far as possible ('internal locus of evaluation').
- Structure and summarise, but without interpreting or analysing the material.

8
Analytic coaching:
In search of insight

There are a thousand unnoticed openings, continued my father,
which let a penetrating eye at once into a man's soul; and I maintain
it, added he, that a man of sense does not lay down his hat in coming
into a room – or take it up in going out of it, but something escapes,
which discovers him.

Laurence Sterne, *The Life and Opinions of
Tristram Shandy Gentleman*

Introduction: psychoanalysis and analytic coaching

In analytic coaching, 'understanding from the inside' is central, in the form
of a joint journey of discovery by coach and coachee. The aim is to
increase the coachee's insight into his or her own issues and problems. The
coach does not pose as an 'expert', or even as someone who has acquired
a large measure of self-knowledge or insight into human nature. The
coach's position is rather that of an 'empiricist' – someone who has
already trodden this path of insight and understanding – and of a
'companion' on the journey of discovery. Preparation for analytic coaching consists mainly of acquiring deep understanding of your own coaching
issues from the inside.[1]

Why is 'insight into your own issues' considered so important? For the
following four reasons in particular:

- Because you can only change yourself, or that which you yourself
  contribute to difficult situations.
- Because 'insight' as such can bring a healthy form of relief – painful
  feelings often *dissolve*[2] when you know where they come from.

1. There are many introductions to the analytic or psychodynamic approach. We
   refer in the text to Freud, its founder, and have also used Brown and Pedder
   (1979), Symington (1986) and Malan (1995), among others.
2. In 'dissolve' the two meanings of the English word 'solution' come surprisingly

- Because obtaining insight is a first necessary step towards *expressing* your feelings, which brings more of that same kind of relief.
- Because insight and expression contribute to the realisation that things are not as 'terrible' as you may have thought before.

Surprisingly, 'learning' is not central in this approach, despite the emphasis on 'insight' and 'understanding'. The aim here is not to 'learn about yourself' ... indeed, as we will see later, this form of learning is considered suspect by analysts. Rather, the aim is to 'learn in yourself': by examining your actions and feelings, identifying the barriers to insight within yourself and reflecting on the effect that enhanced insight has on you.

What is it that we are trying to understand in analytic coaching? To answer this, it is useful to go back to the coachee's initial position, or the problem as it is presented at the outset. That initial position always concerns either:

- something that the coachee has but does not want, or
- something that the coachee does not have but would like.

To put it briefly, in this initial position there is always a degree of conflict. As coaches we start with a *conflict* as often as we start with a new issue, and when we dig deeper we usually find ... a conflict! Conflicts pile on top of each other and exist on several levels:

- To start with, there are often conflicts between myself and my circumstances, or between myself and others.
- Below that level, I often note a conflict within myself, in the form of inconsistencies between opposing needs and tendencies – for example, between 'what I want now' and 'what is good for me', or between my actions and my reasoning.
- Below that level, I note conflicts within deeper layers of myself. What do I actually want? Am I myself working to achieve what I really want? Are there internal barriers preventing me from doing so?

The analytic coach attempts to explore these conflicts between opposing forces; hence *psychodynamic coaching* as an alternative name for analytic coaching, derived from the dynamics of opposing force fields.

The assumption of conflicts within and between layers of our personalities point to contributions from an unconscious part of ourselves, according to the founding fathers of psychoanalysis. This position is debatable, because it assumes the existence of deeper layers that we cannot apprehend – so how do we know that those layers do indeed exist? It is difficult to demonstrate something that we cannot apprehend.[3]

    close together, as Freud (1900) also points out with reference to the German words 'lösung' and 'auflösung' ('resolution' and 'solution').

Phenomena

The analytic approach focuses on everything that can produce deeper insight, as well as on all of the barriers to greater insight. Over the years, various people have listed the psychological phenomena that we may encounter in this approach. Many of these are also mentioned in other approaches, thereby testifying to their debt to the psychoanalytic approach.

Transference

In the relationship between coachee and coach, things happen that also happen between the coachee and others, and between the coach and others. With the coach, the coachee repeats patterns of interaction which (s)he has played out previously with others. These patterns of interaction may shed light on the coachee's expressed problem. This phenomenon of the repetition of patterns originating outside the coaching situation itself was referred to by Freud as *transference* (*Übertragung*). More specifically, when it occurs in the coachee it is known as *transference* and when it occurs in the coach it is known as *counter-transference*.

Transference can often be recognised in disproportionate responses, or in responses which do not seem to bear any relation to what has just been said. It is worth the coach's effort to unravel carefully – and sometimes together with the coachee – 'what' comes from 'whom'. In other words, 'What originates within myself?' and 'What does the other person trigger in me?'

In his early collaboration with Breuer, Freud realised how much insight these transference phenomena can give into the client's problem.[4] Freud and his followers connected transference with formative patterns in a person's life: in other words, patterns within the family in which a person is raised. Transference is therefore usually described as the repetition of patterns of interaction originally played out vis-à-vis parental figures. These days, we see more and more interpretations that refer to current patterns, for example to the coachee's present working relationships (Malan, 1995). Chapter 14 – on 'organisation coaching' – looks in more detail at transference originating in the coachee's organisation.

We see transference as a phenomenon that occurs in virtually every situation in which someone is talking about their own situations or experiences. It starts in fact when someone talks in an agitated manner about something that has led to anger, or gloomily about some disappointment. The coachee

3. Nevertheless, the books and articles in which Freud gathers together the different clues to the existence of an unconscious – in dreams (Freud, 1900), slips of the tongue, slips of the pen, mistakes, forgetfulness and clumsiness (Freud, 1904/1924), jokes (Freud, 1905), works of art (e.g. Freud, 1914b), humour (Freud, 1928), denials (Freud, 1925) and symptoms (Freud, 1926) – are among his most illuminating works.
4. For information on waxing insight in transference, see Breuer and Freud (1895), and Freud (1912b) or (in the entertaining guise of a novel) Yalom (1992).

is not just talking about that situation but, in a way, also expressing him- or herself as if it were being relived. Chapter 11 of *Learning with Colleagues* – on 'reflections of there-and-then in here-and-now' – contains examples of transference in peer consultation groups: behaviour during the session that reflects behaviour from the situation described by the issue holder. Similar reflections occur very easily in coaching conversations.

There are clear indications that the discoverers of transference phenomena, Breuer and Freud, were greatly shocked at first by the power of the (sexually charged) transference that they experienced in the presence of 'Anna O.' and 'Dora' respectively (see, for example, Lear, 2003). Only gradually did Freud become aware of the high value that transference can have in terms of the beneficial impact of therapeutic conversations themselves. It enables coach and coachee to explore together what is happening with them in the present moment. From this, they can gain insight into what is going on within the coachee.

The value of counter-transference – or the feelings and response patterns that the coachee, during the conversation, triggers in the coach – was recognised explicitly only after Freud's death. The first generation of analysts usually saw counter-transference as something that the analyst keeps 'under control'. In these terms, a well-trained analyst continuously 'delivers' the same dispassionate and exploring behaviour, as a firm reminder of the task at hand and as a 'smooth mirror', and thereby to be as open as possible for transference phenomena originating with the client The usefulness of counter-transference in the coaching process itself was only appreciated subsequently. Paula Heimann (1950) was among the first to propose that counter-transference be viewed as a tool for understanding the client better. She suggests that feelings aroused in the therapist be used as a key to deeper understanding of the client, so that the therapist no longer regards the repression or communication of those feelings as the only two alternatives.[5] An analytic coach must be able to listen not only to the coachee, but also to internal reactions and feelings as they arise during the coaching process.

When looking into transference phenomena, it is often useful to consider the following patterns or scenarios:

1. Successful attribution to the other person of a part of oneself, also known as *projective identification* (Klein, 1946). Here, the coachee attributes something to the coach with which the coach can identify. Conversely, the coach attributes something to the coachee with which the coachee can identify.

5. According to Heimann (1950), both of these alternatives have an adverse effect on the quality of the coaching. If counter-transference feelings are repressed the coach would greatly restrict his/her own scope for action; if counter-transference feelings are communicated, however, they would distract coach and coachee from the coaching itself, which should remain focused on the coachee.

2. Attempts to influence the relationship and possibly to undermine the clear division of roles between coach and coachee. This can include:
    –   the desire to experience earlier relationship patterns again and again (*re-enactment*)
    –   the attempt to provoke another party into adopting a different position or a different role.
3. An addition to the process of exploration within the coaching: the transference phenomena add something to the joint verbal exploration (see Freud, 1914a and the examples in Chapter 11 of *Learning with Colleagues*).
4. An addition to the results of the coaching: 'trying out' or 'testing' with the coach of new or almost forgotten patterns of interaction. This often goes by the name of the *corrective emotional experience*, see for example Malan (1995).

The value of the addition of (counter-)transference to the exploration process is particularly hard to overestimate. As coach you can offer considerable added value if you are able to note the initially unconscious transference phenomena, draw attention to them and use them in the exploration with the client.

An example

The coachee and the coach have made a first appointment and the coachee arrives very early. The coachee later admits that she wanted to avoid arriving late at all costs. A revealing start, as it later emerges. The coachee always has the feeling that she is being asked to meet very high standards and is not up to it. She is so afraid of failure that she works away endlessly on reports which she thinks are never good enough. She lacks the nerve to ask colleagues for feedback on her ideas. This recurs in the coaching relationship as well. The coach has a tendency to behave in a similar manner to the coachee. Through her efforts to 'do the right thing', she reinforces the pre-existing pattern in the coachee. The latter feels that her coach is making demands on her and endeavours to meet those demands. She wants to do the right thing for the coach and wants to meet all of her (assumed) expectations. The coach feels that she is treading on eggshells and cannot give any feedback that may come across as overly critical. The coachee starts to talk less, in order to prompt fewer reactions. When the coach points out that relationships at work may be repeating themselves in the coaching relationship, this comes as an enormous relief to the coachee. She can now be herself in the coaching relationship and gradually learns to be a little easier on herself. And so does the coach!

Defences against emerging insight

The coachee is free, even without the coach, to gain a great deal of insight into his or her own issues. However, the coachee often fails to take up these opportunities and does not admit certain insights – or, according to Freud, represses the possibility of insight within the unconscious. It may be that certain insights are unpleasant or painful, that they bring conflicts too close to the surface, or that they stand in the way of certain ways of living and working. If such insights break through into the coaching situation the coachee may, instead of welcoming them, erect all sorts of barriers against them, just as (s)he does outside the coaching context. In the analytic literature, these barriers are known as *defences*.[6] Freud's daughter Anna listed all the defence mechanisms uncovered by her father (Freud, 1936):

1. *Repression*, in which we are unaware, or no longer aware, of unpleasant or unwelcome feelings or experiences. *Suppression* is a more active variant, in which we intentionally try not to think about something.
2. *Regression*: withdrawal from painful situations and difficult responsibilities. In more extreme situations, this can quite literally give rise to a return to childhood behaviour. Harmless examples of this are sleep as regression from our waking existence and holidays as regression from the seriousness of our work. Dissociation and phobic avoidance of certain situations are more extreme variants, as are delusion and depersonalisation.
3. *Reaction formation*: feeling or behaving in a way that is diametrically opposed to the unpleasant fact and to one's own experience. Specific examples include:
   - active *denial* of unpleasant facts or perceptions
   - *rationalising*, by presenting current facts in an unrealistically positive light, or by dismissing them as irrelevant
   - *undoing*, by actually erasing traces of surviving memories, such as photographs and letters, or by changing the narrative when it is recounted
   - *obsessive-neurotic phenomena*, in which we permit ourselves all sorts of rituals and controlling behaviour.
4. *Isolation*: removing an impression or feeling from the context in which it arose.
5. *Projection*: externalising unacceptable feelings by attributing them to others. 'The pot calling the kettle black' is an expression of this.
6. *Introjection*: just as we can externalise unacceptable feelings (projection), we can also attribute positive qualities observed in others to ourselves. The combination of projection and introjection of positive and negative qualities is known as *splitting*.
7. *Displacement* as a way of dealing with unpleasant experiences. Instead of approaching directly a person who has offended us, we take it out on someone else. We may even take out our anger or other negative feelings on ourselves as the 'safest' target: turning against the self.

6.   For the earliest discussion of defence or 'Abwehr', see Freud, 1894 and 1896.

8. *Inversion* of a feeling into its opposite: for example, if we feel power-less we can lose ourselves in daydreams in which we are in control and all-powerful.
9. *Conversion*, in the form of a translation into a physical reaction. Examples can be found in all sorts of psychosomatic, and often stress-related, phenomena.
10. *Sublimation:* using the emotional energy released by frustration or unpleasant feelings towards 'higher ends', such as creative and altruistic work. This is a defence which is seen as very positive in a social context and may lead to positive results.

Clearly, these defences cannot be considered independently of each other, and basic defensive reactions such as repression and projection may give rise in a subsequent phase to other, more subtle defences[7] – especially when the pressure increases and new, unpleasant insights and feelings present themselves.

An example[8]

Coachees often talk about their relationships with their managers. For example, when a coachee expresses dislike of a boss, this is an unambigu-ous expression of an unpleasant feeling and so probably not a defence. Or perhaps it is after all a *displacement* of an inexpressible dislike of another, much more significant person in the coachee's life: (s)he might actually want to say: 'I don't know how to deal with my father and therefore I can't stand people in authority.'

A coachee may raise a dislike of the boss in another way, as a defence:

- *Repression:* 'I wonder why I often feel so tired and tense at work.'
- *Suppression:* 'I am irritated with my boss but I don't know why.'
- *Regression* (dissociation): 'I'm always telling my boss stupid jokes.'
- *Reaction formation* (denial): 'My boss is irrelevant to me.'
- *Reaction formation* (rationalisation): 'My boss still has a lot to learn about managing.'
- *Reaction formation* (acting out): 'Without thinking about what I was doing, I smashed my computer by throwing it on the floor.'
- *Isolation:* 'I don't agree with my boss's strategic plan.'
- *Projection:* 'My boss doesn't like me.'

7. Within reaction formation in particular, there are many interesting and complicated defences, such as *acting out* (converting one's own impulses into behaviour without thinking), *intellectualising* (giving oneself over to abstract thinking) or *learning* (merely understanding what is happening without converting that understanding into a response). These are defences that we often encounter during coaching.
8. The idea for this example comes from Vaillant (1992)

- *Introjection:* 'Strange that it should be my boss who made me realise how well I'm actually doing.'
- *Displacement:* 'I don't like that bootlicking colleague.'
- *Displacement* (turning against the self; passive aggression): 'I don't like myself"
- *Inversion:* 'I love my boss.'
- *Conversion:* 'Yesterday I spent another day with my boss (...) Later I went home with a fever.'
- *Sublimation:* 'I rewrote my boss's strategic plan and had it approved by him and the board of management.'
- *Sublimation* (to altruism): 'I have become the works council mediator for people who have trouble with the style of management in this organisation.'

Approaches to analytic coaching

Traditional approach

Historically, analysts have not been keen to prescribe or to follow fixed procedures. However, Freud wrote six 'technical papers' (Freud, 1912–15 inclusive) which we can draw on for advice on to how to proceed as an analytic coach. The papers start from the analyst's basic rule which states that coachees undertake to share everything that comes into their head,

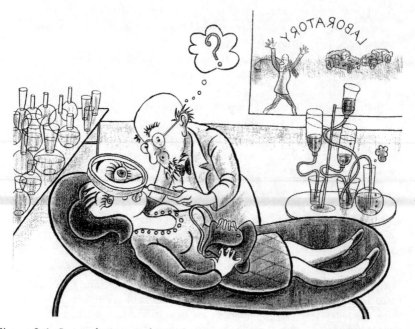

Figure 8.1 In analytic coaching the coachee submits to a thorough examination, and defends him or herself against it

without censorship or selectivity. The coachee talks and associates freely and easily, so providing 'material' that can be analysed. The analytic coach reflects this basic rule with a receptivity that accepts all of the material, also without censoring or selecting. The coach practises an 'evenly hovering attention' ('gleichschwebende Aufmerksamkeit' – Freud, 1912c), which listens to everything without censure. The aim is to receive information without focusing one's own attention on specific points or being concerned, for example, about whether something that has already emerged is significant or needs to be analysed further. The coach trusts that insight will come of itself, from the coach's 'unconscious memory'. The intention is, therefore, that the 'giving unconscious' of the coachee should come into contact as closely as possible with the 'receiving unconscious' of the coach.

As the coach, you seek to disconnect yourself from your memory and your desires,[9] in order to be as fully present as possible in the here and now with the coachee. You end up with a negative capability (Bion, 1970) – the ability to be in situations where uncertainty, ambiguity and doubt prevail, without making laborious attempts to get out of them, for example via the route of statements of facts, interpretations and solutions.

An example

(The coachee is talking about a difficult client with whom she is just not making any headway) '… it's like walking through treacle. He is so ambitious but so quiet at the same time, almost timid, but not very aware of his own impact. He's not my type of person … he works on the trading floor, isn't really interested in people …' 'Your type of person? What do you mean?' 'He has a tendency to be controlling, to keep a tight grip on everything, so we're unable to complete the project. It is unbelievably frustrating. I just feel confusion when I think about him … What am I to do with that man? In fact, I feel confused now as well.' 'What does his "type" remind you of?' 'What? What does he remind me of? Perhaps he reminds me most of my brother …' (Talks about her brother, and suddenly interrupts herself) '… perhaps I am avoiding something here. Maybe I have the same sort of rivalry with that client as I do with my brother? Phew … Isn't life difficult sometimes? There aren't many people as difficult as my brother …' 'You said that you're feeling the same confusion in this conversation as well …?'

Another attempt to sum up in a word what is expected of the coach in analytic coaching is *containment* (Bion, 1963). The aim is quite literally to act like a vessel to 'contain' the problem presented by the coachee, including the

---

9. Bion (1970) refers to an active *elimination* of memory and desires, and even of sensory impressions and understanding, in order to be able to free attention for the emotional quality of the client's 'material'.

accompanying emotions, so that it becomes possible for the coachee to transform the emotions and gain new insight into their own defences. This containment helps the coachee to pause and reflect at precisely those moments when strong emotions or difficult issues are in the room. Containment offers space to think about these emotions and issues, and keeps boundaries around that thinking space to protect it from tendencies to move away to other, safer issues which are, again, defences to emerging insight.

Containment places great demands on the coach:

- not just remaining calm and neutral in an emotionally charged situation
- but also accepting the widest possible range of expressions and accompanying emotions
- while using one's own emotions, which are often triggered unconsciously by the coachee's emotions
- and intervening on the basis of one's own emotions, without actually expressing them as emotions (Heimann, 1950)
- and being able at the same time to offer clear and firm boundaries on the coaching relationship – the coach offers exceptional acceptance, but only within the limits of the coaching, outside which that availability disappears.

The coach usually finds indications of conflicts and defences in the coachee's material, which also express themselves in transference as *resistance* to the analysis and to the coach.[10] The difficult task of the coach is to bring these conflicts and resistances, and this transference, to the surface. This requires a considerable courage – not only to look for snags, omissions and discrepancies in the coachee's story, but also (and even more) to explore the coach's own relationship with the coachee out loud. This also requires a great deal of experience, and the ability to communicate possible insights into conflicts and hidden forms of resistance in a measured way that is manageable for the coachee.

The aim of analytic coaching is to shine the light of insight on what the coachee has repressed and kept to him- or herself and thereby to overcome internal defences and resistance (Freud, 1914a). Analysts have become fairly strict in terms of their methodology to achieve this. Freud, too, after an informal, exploratory start, made his own contribution. The now 'traditional' psychoanalysis is intensive and thorough, with four to six sessions a week taking place over a period of years, the arrangement with a couch where the coachee is unable to see the coach, and a long period of training for analysts as analysands and as physicians (although Freud himself was never keen to impose the latter obligation). Freud defended the spatial arrangement with the

10. Freud (1912b) points out that in virtually every case where the basic rule becomes difficult for the coachee, and free association thus breaks down, there is something going on within the coachee that is connected with the person of the coach. This illustrates just how strong transference is.

couch by saying, among other things, that he did not want to be stared at all day (Freud, 1913). Crucially, of course, this arrangement allows considerably more scope for free association and transference.

The ladder of inference

A tried and tested method to stimulate insight in a coaching conversation is described in Argyris (1990). It is designed to facilitate moving the coachee away from complaining and finding fault in others or in external causes and towards his or her own stake in the problem, Argyris is not, like Freud, looking for unconscious motivations. He starts with something that all of the defences described above have in common, and that their existence discloses: the fact that something unpleasant has been warded off or kept at a safe distance. The unpleasant feeling or problem has been 'dealt with' or 'processed' in a defensive manner. The experience with even the beginnings of increasing insight was experienced as unpleasant, disagreeable or even intolerable, and so was brushed aside. Conclusions have been arrived at and the defence is the result. In practice, this usually results in the coachee taking action on the basis of his or her own first impression, without first going over scenarios, alone or together with the coach. It is as if the coachee is climbing a ladder very quickly, missing out the occasional rung: a ladder that runs from a specific event, to the impressions it makes, to the emotions, to the interpretations, to the conclusions, and finally to the actions.

In this analytic approach, coachee and coach slowly go back down the ladder of inference and attempt to return to the situation that preceded the

Figure 8.2 The ladder of inference can expose new insights

defences: in other words, before the current situation in which everything appears to be 'resolved'. Put another way, the question is: 'How can we, nevertheless, gain insight from that first, painful event? How can we find other interpretations/draw other conclusions/prepare other courses of action?' Much too often, we assume that (Senge et al., 1994):

- our actions are well-founded in our convictions
- our convictions are *the* truth
- our convictions are based on real data
- the reality is clear
- the data that we select are the (only) real data.

A coach using the ladder of inference goes about it as follows. On the basis of a statement or question from the coachee, (s)he tries to identify the underlying conflict that generated the negative experience. The coach tries to adopt as independent a position as possible. The procedure is roughly as follows:[11]

1. The coachee presents a concern or problem – something (s)he is having trouble with or wants to resolve.
2. Together with the coachee, the coach looks at the way in which the concern or problem has been formulated – what sort of conclusions or assumptions are evident? For example, the coach looks at the descriptions of self and others. What does the coachee seem to emphasize, and what appears to have been left out?
3. The coach considers personally what these assumptions are based on. What are the observations or impressions that lead the coachee to draw these conclusions? In this step we sometimes come close to the source of the defences. If not – if no powerful, painful observations or impressions come to the fore – the coach can ask about associations, or about intuitions that support the assumptions. These may even be things that seem not directly relevant here. The more spontaneous, the better.
4. The coach endeavours to keep the conflict that has now emerged – the unpleasant impressions, the contradictions, the offences, the fragility of the coachee, and so on – the focus of the conversation. The coachee is often tempted to respond to this by releasing a new defence: a rationalisation perhaps, or a strongly intellectualising label, or perhaps a projection vis à vis the coach. But this is precisely the moment that can produce insight. However painful it may be, it is worth sticking with it and examining it a bit longer.

11. This procedure has similarities with the U METHOD from *Learning with colleagues* (Chapter 4) and with some RET approaches. One difference is that these two approaches attempt to replace the assumptions with other, more 'appropriate', 'rational' assumptions. This makes these methods much more directive.

5. Finally, there is time for a critical review of the assumptions referred to above (Step 2). Often, the defences (generalisations, attributions, repressions, rationalisations, and so on) do not stand up to careful examination. The coach now asks: 'What other assumptions might you make?' Coach and coachee seek out alternative assumptions which can serve as a provisional point of departure, rather than a new way of defining and 'fixing' the issue.

Summary: analytic coaching

Analytic coaching is a form of coaching in which:

- Coach and coachee work towards increasing insight into the coachee's problem.
- Coach and coachee work with internal conflicts within the coachee and the resulting defences and resistance.
- The aim is to overcome defences and resistance, in order to gain insight into factors that were previously less obvious.

Psychological phenomena investigated in analytic coaching:

- Defences as barriers to enhanced insight, such as repression, regression, reaction formation, isolation, projection, introjection, displacement, inversion, conversion and sublimation.
- Transference as a carrier wave for defences to become visible as resistance to the coaching process and to the coach.

We introduce two different analytic approaches:

- Traditional analytic coaching, in which the basic rule is to share everything without censure or selection (coachee) and to receive everything without censure or selection (coach). Moreover, the coach offers evenly hovering attention and containment.
- More cognitive analytic coaching: the ladder of inference in which, in a more systematic, directive manner, statements are investigated with a view to identifying assumptions, perceptions and underlying conflicts.

9

Paradoxical coaching: Moving with defences

> [Change does not exist, for] what would be in change changes neither in the shape it is in nor in the shape it is not in.
>
> Zeno of Elea, Fragment DK 29B4

Introduction: the 'difficult' coachee

The paradoxical approach is eminently suited to tricky coaching situations in which 'things are not going smoothly'; where, for example:

- The coachee does not appear to accept the coach whole-heartedly.
- Initiatives appear to get bogged down.
- In one way or another, the coach feels constantly challenged – to be a better coach or to give more, less, or cleverer advice.

When coaching is going well, there is harmony between coachee and coach. The coachee has a real problem or questions; the coach possesses real expertise and authority – also in the eyes of the coachee! – and there is a willingness on the part of the coachee to be coached and on the part of the coach to coach. When things are not going smoothly, invariably one or more of these conditions are not being met, though other conditions may well be – if this were not the case, then the coaching relationship would have been discontinued. Things may not go smoothly because the coach does not feel capable or motivated to coach, in which case it is time to refer the coachee to someone else. But it may also be because the coachee does not meet some of the conditions and is therefore sending out ambiguous messages. This can happen overtly or less overtly. Signs of this may include:

- 'I don't have a problem' (e.g. by referring to others who 'do have a problem').
- 'Nothing can be changed here' (e.g. by emphasising the extent and complexity of the situation, or by referring to one's own powerlessness).

- 'I doubt your expertise' (e.g. by saying that the coach doesn't understand, or doesn't understand well enough, or by suggesting that (s)he is not offering useful advice or appropriate interventions).

All of these signals are completely reasonable and understandable but, within the coaching relationship, they have a *paradoxical* significance: the coachee is evidently appealing to the coach to look at his or her concerns and problems, but simultaneously undermining that appeal. The paradoxical signal is that within an appeal for help and influence, there is simultaneously an undeniable appeal to leave the coachee alone or to let everything carry on as usual. In this situation, nothing the coach can do is ever good enough: helping is good but not all good, and not helping is good but not all good. In the literature this is known as the *double bind* (Watzlawick et al., 1967): the coachee double-binds the coach using contradictory requests and, simultaneously, exerting pressure (coming from the contract, an on-going relationship, or even a threat) to make progress. A confusing, frustrating and dispiriting dilemma, but one that we have all experienced as coaches at some time.

Ambiguous communication

The paradoxical approach claims to provide an answer to dilemmas of this type and says that it is necessary, in these situations, for the coach to start sending out ambiguous signals as well. The coach thereby puts the coachee under pressure to resolve the dilemma personally. The paradoxical approach is extremely *directive*: not only within the coaching, which employs directive interventions, but also within the coaching relationship, which the coach puts to the test. Another feature of the paradoxical approach is that it is above all *interactional*: it focuses less on the problem and its background than on the interaction between the coachee and others, specifically the coach. The aim is to influence this interaction in such a way that it becomes less ambiguous.

The main paradoxical technique is the 'utilisation technique' (Erickson, 1959): instead of persevering with a more or less overt conflict, the coach starts to (counter-intuitively!) utilise the specific characteristics of the difficult interaction, in such a way that the coach helps the coachee to:

- take more responsibility for her own behaviour, even if that behaviour consists of such 'negative' things like symptoms, moaning, ambiguities or resistance
- introduce and test alternatives to the coachee's current patterns of behaviour.

The utilisation technique does this by, first, inviting the coachee to continue doing the same, second, requesting more of the same, or third, suggesting the same thing in new guises. In fact, the coach puts the coachee in a paradox-ical situation that cannot be resolved as long as the coachee continues to undermine a productive coaching relationship. All examples of 'utilisation technique' are ambiguous and paradoxical, because the coach accepts all of the coachee's resistance to the coaching relationship *while remaining present and available in that relationship as the coach*. The coach therefore reacts paradoxically to the coachee's paradoxical behaviour.

Paradoxical coaching approaches

Well-known applications of utilisation technique (Haley, 1963) include the the ones we will work through in the following example.

> *An example*
>
> A manager has received disappointing reactions from her own staff to the distribution of a 360° feedback form ('You don't spend enough time with us'; 'You're not in the department very much and seem more inter-ested in the external, ceremonial aspects of being a manager', and so on). She takes this feedback very much to heart. She calls in a coach but, right from the outset, displays little confidence and is despondent about her own prospects: 'I'll never be a good manager'; 'This is going nowhere ...'

1. *Positive labelling* of symptoms and problems as well as of the resistant behaviour itself. A positive motive, and sometimes a positive result, is consistently attributed to the apparently negative behaviour. The coach emphasises the positive side of the problem and the advantages associated with the current situation. In fact, the coach accepts and confirms all of the coachee's behaviour, including the behaviour that is undermining the coaching itself.

> *Example, continued*
>
> The coach says that the manager is just showing that her heart is very much in it by representing the department so often, and that she is doing the right thing by treating her staff as independent adults and not trying to 'pamper' them too much. And that it is very professional of her to call in a coach. It is precisely by *not* always running after people that you can take time to be a great manager. Furthermore, the very fact that the manager is dispirited is interpreted by the coach as a sign that her heart is in it.

2. *Prescribing problems and resistance*. The coach suggests that the 'difficult' or 'problematic' behaviour be displayed more, even extended, and applied in more situations. Coach and coachee can also make agreements about

planning and applying the same behaviour more frequently, so that the coachee can get an (even firmer) grip on it.

Example, continued
The coach says: 'In my view you would do best to be present even less, so as to become an even better manager. Moreover, they don't accept you anyway, so concentrate on the tasks that you prefer and that you do best.'

3. *Eliciting change through surprises.* The coach does not react 'congruently' to the behaviour presented, but incongruently: instead of going along with the usual patterns of interaction (for example by offering help, or wearing herself out), the coach opts for the unexpected. (S)he intervenes in surprising ways and introduces new situations and circumstances.

Example, continued
'Perhaps it would be a good idea to have your staff distribute a 360° survey of their own. Then you can tell them what you think of them!'

4. *Negotiating en route to the 'continuum of change'.* Knowing that a small step in the right direction sometimes makes a big difference, the coach makes a proposal for a minuscule change, usually as an experiment and often merely a change in an irrelevant aspect of the problem situation. Negotiating techniques can be used here: 'To what extent are you prepared to try something different?'; 'When would you be prepared to change?', and so on.

Example, continued
'What's more, while you're still managing the department and before you're finally rejected by your staff, you can also experiment with 'attention', in preparation for your next job as a manager. I wonder if anything will change if, for example, you maintain eye contact for one second longer each time you meet someone. Do you think they will notice the difference?'

5. *Posing the counter-paradox.* The most powerful intervention, in which the coach him or herself poses a similar unsolvable dilemma for the coachee. The coach creates a situation which is unpleasant for the coachee, one from which (s)he can escape only with unambiguous behaviour. The most common application of this is the (apparently) realistic assertion that no change or improvement is likely, so that the coachee herself feels called upon to 'prove' that something better is indeed possible.

Example, continued

'And perhaps we can extrapolate the experiment to this coaching situation, because this will come to an end too of course – there will come a day when I reject you as my coachee. How far could you take things with me? You could turn up late next time, or forget the appointment, or talk absent-mindedly as if your thoughts are elsewhere. And then ask me for feedback.'

Two variations: ironic and provocative

There are two further variations on this directive, ambiguous and interactional path, one of which is less severely manipulative and directive, while the other goes even further than the paradoxical approach. The gentler variation is the *ironic approach* (de Haan, 1999) and the more radical variation is the *provocative approach* (Farrelly and Brandsma, 1974).

The *ironic approach* resembles ordinary directive coaching. The coach offers frequent, honest and sound advice within the context of the coachee's

Figure 9.1 Paradoxical coaching sometimes finds completely unexpected, almost magical, answers to the coachee's questions

question while simultaneously *hinting* at quite different advice outside that context. The advice is therefore communicated ambiguously, with the suggestion that other kinds of advice might also be given. This prompts the coachee to think carefully about what 'the ironic coach' actually means. Due to its ambiguity, irony provides a strong incentive to independent thought on the part of the coachee. At the same time, it is a gentler intervention than the paradoxical approach because you do not encourage the coachee to do something really unusual, such as repeating and amplifying symptomatic behaviour.

> *Example, continued*
> 'It strikes me that your staff are only able to talk about you in a 360° feedback survey. Are they so intimidated by you that they can only say that they want to see more of you by means of a questionnaire? You must really keep them under your thumb! Or is something else going on?'

The *provocative approach*, on the other hand, is an exaggeration or enlargement of the paradoxical approach. The coach is now truly a Devil's advocate who provokes, challenges and derides the coachee in every possible way. The coach becomes a sort of court jester who uses gallows humour and applies a *reductio ad absurdum* to all the coachee's behaviour, making it appear more and more ridiculous. The intention behind this rather tormenting approach (coachees must first sign a document confirming that they agree to this provocative method!) is to mobilise as much of the coachee's resilience as possible. This approach toughens up and strengthens the coachee: if the coachee can stand up to the provocative coach, life in the work situation will no longer pose any problems either, so the thinking goes.

Provocative utilisation techniques include the following:

6. *Drawing out resistance.* In provocative coaching, the 'difficult' situation with ambiguous messages from the coachee is precisely the situation that is desired, so the coach attempts to engineer that situation as quickly as possible, for example by saying: 'There is an enormous problem here', 'I'm not really an expert' or 'Really everything needs to change here'. (Compare these statements with the three conditions for coaching at the start of this chapter).

> *Example, continued*
> 'But that is terrible. The last time I "treated" a manager with such a feedback profile it led via the works council to a case before the senior management. The manager was sacked on the spot and hasn't worked since. I'm none too optimistic for you. What can you still do to conceal these feedback results from the rest of the organisation?'

7. *Jokes, anecdotes and associations.* The coach seizes the initiative in the conversation by talking animatedly about his or her own past and all sorts of interesting previous coachees. In addition, the coach introduces a joke or a strange, exaggerated association each time the coachee makes a contribution to the conversation.

    ### Example, continued
    'This isn't great for me either. I can't always be associated with coachees who lose their jobs, unless I can attribute the dismissal to myself of course. What do you think about us drafting a letter of resignation for you together now, saying something like: "After carefully studying the feedback from my staff I decided that I was not up to the job of manager. My coach made me realise that, for my future career, I would do well to aspire to a purely ceremonial position."'

8. *Interrupting and frustrating* the coachee's story. In fact, the coach does not even allow the coachee to present a problem or initial question at the start of the conversation. Sometimes, the coachee doesn't get halfway through a sentence before the coach is shouting 'You look funny today!' or 'Did you brush your hair this morning?' Interruptions and discouragements of this type remain a permanent part of the coaching.

According to practitioners of these three coaching approaches, which are all *manipulative* in nature, all other coaching approaches are also manipulative, though their practitioners don't always admit it. The non-directive, person-centred opening, for example, which states explicitly that the coach will not influence the coachee (see Chapter 7), is in fact very paradoxical and manipulative because the coachee is specifically entering this relationship in order to request influence from the coach. Paradoxical coaches say that the most important ingredient of any effective coaching is the fact that the coachee does not gain control over the coach (see the marvellous epilogue about 'one-upmanship' in Haley, 1963).

Summary: paradoxical coaching

Paradoxical coaching is a form of coaching in which:

- The ambiguity in the coachee's presentation of the problem is central.
- The coach answers that ambiguity with his or her own ambiguity vis-à-vis the coachee.
- The coach intentionally influences the patterns of interaction between coachee and coach.

The paradoxical coach approaches the coachee with utilisation techniques that utilise the coachee's difficult behaviour, such as:

- positive labelling of the coachee's symptoms and problems
- prescribing new problems and resistance
- eliciting changes by surprising assignments
- negotiating with the coachee about the extent to which (s)he is going to change
- posing the 'counter-paradox'.

An alternative, gentler form of paradoxical coaching is ironic coaching: the coach gives advice but also suggests that different advice is possible, or deliberately introduces doubt about the advice (s)he is giving.

An alternative, more radical form of paradoxical coaching is provocative coaching: the coach deliberately provokes resistance and frustrates the coachee's thought processes. Examples of provocative coaching techniques include:

- drawing out resistance by exaggerating the problem
- jokes, anecdotes and associations at the coachee's expense
- interrupting and frustrating the coachee's story.

10
Coaching methodologies

Every coach, consciously or unconsciously, uses certain *conversational models*, or established ways of developing a coaching conversation. In this chapter, the different approaches to coaching conversations introduced in the previous four chapters are summarised as conversational models in terms of specific methods for use in coaching conversations. Bear in mind that the non-directive approaches to coaching cannot be summarised in step-by-step methods – by definition, such conversations are structured not by the coach, but by the coachee. In two of the following methods, the ANALYTIC METHOD and the COUNSELLING METHOD, therefore, no formal steps are indicated. The suggested approaches are as specific as possible and can be used by the coach in facilitating the coachee. It is also advisable to work with one of the

Figure 10.1 A step-by-step coaching method gives the coach the opportunity
to observe the coachee while she is hard at work

methods *explicitly*, putting it on the table during coaching: this creates a situation where coach and coachee regularly and explicitly reflect on their process in the here-and-now, which can be very effective.

The methods necessarily simplify the coaching approaches that we have described before. In principle, each method shows how to handle a single issue or problem, while coaching conversations generally involve the handling of several, intertwined issues on many levels. Moreover, we often set aside the last few minutes of every coaching conversation for a short review, something that does not feature in every method.

Two of the conversational models illustrated below have been published previously: the GROW METHOD in Whitmore (1992) and the IRONIC METHOD in de Haan (1999). Some methods display similarities with the consultation methods in *Learning with Colleagues* (Chapter 4). In particular, the SOLUTION-FOCUSED METHOD displays similarities with the LEARNING FROM SUCCESS METHOD and the LADDER METHOD – inspired by Argyris (1990) – shows some similarities with the U METHOD.

The GROW method

Step	Description	Time
Step 1	*Presentation of the problem* Coachee introduces his/her issue briefly.	1 min
Step 2	*G: Goal* Coach asks about the goal for the issue *and* for this session: • What do you want to achieve, and when? • What do you want to achieve with me now? • To what extent is that goal specific/challenging/attainable measurable? N.B.: avoid negatively-worded goals.	5 mins
Step 3	*R: Reality* Coach asks about the current state of affairs: • What have you done about it so far, and with what results? N.B.: do not ask any 'how' or 'why' questions at this stage.	5 mins
Step 4	*O: Options* Coach asks about the options open to the coachee: • What options do you have? • What are the pros and cons of the different options? N.B.: when you seem to have all the possible options, ask for just one more.	10 mins
Step 5	*W: Will* Coach asks about the option, or combination of options, that the coachee is going to put into practice: • What are you going to do, and when? • Does that meet your goal? And what about the goal of this conversation? • What obstacles do you expect and how are you going to overcome them? • What resources do you need and how are you going to get them? • Indicate on a scale from 1 to 10 how likely it is that you will carry out that action.	5 mins
	Time needed	26 mins

The solution-focused method[1]

Step	Description	Time
Step 1	*Presentation of the problem* Coachee briefly introduces his/her issue and what has already been tried. The coach asks in particular about what was useful, and what helped.	5 mins
Step 2	*Miracle question* Coach asks about indicators of improvement: how can the coachee check that an improvement has actually taken place? What exactly will be different at that moment?	5 mins
Step 3	*Exceptions* Coach asks about times when the problem does not arise: what are those times like? What happens then? What is the situation like exactly? *Option*: Coach asks for a rating of progress at the present time, on a scale from 0 (no change) to 10 (issue has been completely resolved).	10 mins
Step 4	*Suggestions* Coach gives positive feedback, and suggestions for creating more of that sort of 'exception'.	5 mins
	Contracting Coachee says what (s)he wants to do next and how. The coach assigns 'homework' and explains the rationale behind it. Coach and coachee make a new appointment to review the situation.	10 mins
	Time needed	35 mins

1. Within 'appreciative inquiry' there is a similar structure, the *4-D model* (Cooperrider and Whitney, 2002):

   - *Discover:* discovering in a structured way when the coachee is at his/her best.
   - *Dream:* a dream in which the situation from the first step ('discover') is the norm rather than an exception.
   - *Design:* together with the coach, working towards the realisation of the dream with specific plans.
   - *Deliver:* making arrangements about how to put the plans into practice.

   Discover corresponds to Step 1, Dream to Step 2, Design to Step 4 and Deliver to Step 5 of the SOLUTION-FOCUSED METHOD.

The counselling method

N.B.: this is not a step-by-step method in the usual sense. The scheme presented here merely indicates what types of intervention can be used by the coach. It is the coachee, rather than the coach, who determines what stage the process is at, at any given time. Nor can any indication of time be given, because the coachee decides personally when to move on.

Option	Description	Time
Option 1	*Introduction* The coachee starts the conversation, in the way (s)he wishes.	?
Option 2	*Invitation to explore* The coach adopts an inviting and available stance, but without applying pressure to say more or to explain any particular aspects.	?
Option 3	*Broadening* The coach broadens the issue by summarising and by reflecting feelings. The coach also tries to paraphrase 'between the lines' – stimulating awareness of attitudes, values, etc. – and asks the occasional open question.	?
Option 4	*Reinforcing contact* The coach increases the contact with the coachee by reflecting on the contact itself and by means of self-disclosure: how the coach feels at this moment and how (s)he is involved at this moment.	?
Option 5	*Review* Coach and coachee review the session together and try to describe how they feel following the conversation.	?
	Time needed	?

The analytic and organisation coach method

N.B.: this is not a step-by-step method in the usual sense. The scheme presented here merely indicates what types of intervention can be used by the coach. It is the coachee, rather than the coach, who determines what stage the process is at, at any given time. Nor can any indication of time be given, because the coachee him-/herself decides how long to devote to any one subject – although the coach often monitors the overall length of the session when using this approach.

Option	Description	Time
Option 1	*Introduction* The coachee starts the conversation, in the way (s)he wishes, as far as possible using the basic rule that (s)he can voice anything, including fancies and thoughts that arise in the moment, without selection or criticism. The coach listens, also without selection or criticism. The coach asks him/herself: 'What sorts of signal am I picking up?'	?
Option 2	*Background* The coach looks out for what may lie behind the coachee's spoken words, as well as for assumptions implicit in the coachee's story. The coach is also sensitive to what the coachee leaves out. The coach asks him/herself: 'What is not being said?'	?
Option 3	*Obstacles to insight* The coach explores with the coachee what obstacles there are to incipient insight; what conflicts may be playing a role in the background; and how the coachee attempts to keep those conflicts and other unpleasant feelings out of his/her consciousness and out of the conversation. The coach asks him/herself: 'What conflict do I see?'	?
Option 4	*Transference* The coach explores with the coachee what obstacles there are to gaining fresh insight in the course of this conversation, and what conflicts and resistance are emerging in this conversation. The coach asks him/herself: 'What does the coachee want from me?'	?
	Time needed	Fixed

Extension for the organisation coach method

Option 4a	*Organisation transference* The coach explores with the coachee what barriers existing within the coachee's organisation might resist fresh insights, and what role the coachee 'automatically' takes on. The coach asks him/herself: 'How does the coachee's organisation want the coachee to feel now?'	?

The ladder method

Step	Description	Time
Step 1	*Presentation of the problem* The coachee presents an issue or problem and provides an explanation as necessary.	5–10 mins
Step 2	*Assumptions* Coach and coachee look together at this formulation: what conclusions or assumptions emerge? What attributions does the coachee make, what does (s)he take for granted?	5–10 mins
Step 3	*Motivation for the assumptions* Coach and coachee explore together the bases of these conclusions. What observations or experiences led the coachee to make these assumptions? *Alternative*: The coachee undertakes a free association in relation to the assumptions: what do they remind him/her of?	5–10 mins
Step 4	*Underlying conflict* Coach and coachee explore together what the 'issue behind the issue' is: what problem or deeper conflict lies behind the problem presented? To what extent do the identified assumptions play a role in creating the problem?	5–10 mins
Step 5	*Testing the assumptions* Coach and coachee consider what different assumptions they could make.	5–10 mins
Step 6	*Alternative presentation of the problem* Coach and coachee explore what this means for the nature of the problem.	5–10 mins
Step 7	*Review* Coach and coachee review this conversation together and try to describe what insights they have gained from it.	5–10 mins
	Time needed	35–65 mins

The ironic method

Step	Description	Time
Step 1	*Presentation of the problem* The coachee presents an issue or problem and explains it if necessary.	10 mins
Step 2	*Reformulation as a dilemma* The coach attempts to reformulate the issue as a dilemma, in which an internal contradiction or discrepancy comes to the surface: 'The coachee wants to ... but feels held back by ...'; or 'The coachee wants to put an end to ... but is aware that ...'	10 mins
Step 3	*The ironic intervention* The ironic communication itself. This can consist of a strong emphasis on an aspect of the dilemma that the coach wants to query. Alternatively, the coach can contribute his/her own point of view and place it in a different perspective at the same time. Example: 'Listening to your enthusiastic story, I am strangely reminded of something which went quite wrong last week. But I imagine that it is quite irrelevant in this situation.'	10 mins
Step 4	*Working through* The coach monitors the coachee's response attentively and tries to facilitate this response as much as possible, by means of invitations, open questions or summaries. The coach will summarise the coachee's response to the ironic intervention, without removing the ambiguity of the irony.	15 mins
	Time needed	45 mins

The paradoxical method

Step	Description	Time
Step 1	*Presentation of the problem* The coachee presents an issue or problem and explains it if necessary. The coach helps to make the problem as specific and verifiable as possible and attempts to reformulate the problem for him/herself in terms of a dilemma.	10 mins
Step 2	*Positive labelling* The coach looks for as many positive aspects and motives as possible in the coachee's behaviour in the problem situation. If there are any defences or resistance, the coach accepts and encourages them.	10 mins
Step 3	*Paradoxical instruction* The coach formulates an assignment for the coachee that also contains a dilemma. This new dilemma is designed in such a way that it reflects the initial dilemma, and thereby invites the coachee to persist with both aspects of the initial dilemma. N.B.: a break for reflection is often necessary before the coach can find a suitable paradoxical instruction; Step 3 then takes place in a subsequent coaching conversation.	10 mins
Step 4	*Contracting for the future* Coach and coachee look to the future and the completion of the paradoxical instruction, the coach providing further encouragement.	15 mins
	Time needed	45 mins

Summary: coaching methodologies

The following coaching methods are introduced:

- the GROW METHOD
- the SOLUTION-FOCUSED METHOD
- the COUNSELLING METHOD
- the ANALYTIC METHOD and the ORGANISATION COACH METHOD
- the LADDER METHOD
- the IRONIC METHOD
- the PARADOXICAL METHOD.

Together, these coaching methods cover the entire window of coaching, from exploring to suggesting and from supporting to confronting, including the four different approaches:

1. Problem-focused: GROW METHOD, PARADOXICAL METHOD and IRONIC METHOD.
2. Solution-focused: SOLUTION-FOCUSED METHOD.
3. Person-focused: COUNSELLING METHOD.
4. Insight-focused: ANALYTIC METHOD, ORGANISATION COACH METHOD and LADDER METHOD.

11

Choosing the right method

> The more the therapist is able to tolerate the anxiety of not know-
> ing, the less need is there for the therapist to embrace orthodoxy.
> The creative members of an orthodoxy, any orthodoxy, ultimately
> outgrow their disciplines.
>
> Irvin Yalom, *Love's Executioner*

In this chapter we offer suggestions for using the different coaching approaches and methods and the conversations within which they can be applied. We start with a summary of conclusions from research into the effects of coaching and psychotherapy, which quickly refutes the myth that there is a single 'right' method for every coaching issue, or even for one specific issue. Then we take a look at the evidence from research and practical experience that argues for or against certain methods. This evidence gives rise to recommendations as to the choice of method. However, our main recommendation is to choose a method that fits as closely as possible with your own personality, and to keep exploring and developing that 'personal' method on an on-going basis.

An example

She's a woman in a 'macho' organisation with an abrasive business culture. She didn't have the chance to go to university – her parents thought it unnecessary – but she is clever and has progressed from administrative worker to insurance specialist. Her husband has been unable to keep up with her progress. He trivialises what she does and would prefer that she stay at home with the children. She feels little understood by those around her, including her boss. Her boss notices that sometimes she freezes completely when they are discussing her work. At those times she feels undervalued by him, but doesn't dare to say so. They are unable to work it out together and he refers her to a coach.

The coach might have chosen a provocative approach by trivialising her contributions even more, which could have helped the coachee find her strength through anger. The coach opts for a different, more person-centred approach, however. The coachee talks about her work a lot and slowly her feelings, which fluctuated from feeling superior to feeling injured, develop into a growing self-confidence. The coach helps her to prepare for a performance appraisal with her boss, in which she stands up for herself and says what is bothering her. She asks explicitly for more appreciation for her work, and for a rise in salary. It works: she gains greater recognition from her boss – though the boss doesn't refer anyone to that coach again.

What do we know about the effectiveness of coaching?

There is little quantitative research into the effectiveness of coaching. For a detailed summary of the literature, including a total of seven empirical research articles, see Kampa-Kokesch and Anderson (2001); for a more recent article, see Wasylyshyn (2003).

Most empirical articles about coaching are concerned with the value of coaching from the perspective of the coachee. These articles are often written by coaches themselves and therefore serve partly to account for the quality of their own work. The articles seldom consider control groups – managers or

Figure 11.1 Because we still know so little about the effectiveness of coaching, choosing the right coach and the right approach is often still mainly a matter of taste and following advertising slogans

professionals in the same circumstances who are not being coached. Usually, the research takes the form of an extensive evaluation among the coachees; occasionally coachees even estimate how much their coaching has contributed to the organisation in financial terms. McGovern et al. (2001) worked with a group of 100 managers in 67 organisations who were coached for between six and 12 months. They found that the vast majority of participants were very satisfied with the coaching. In addition, they found that the coaching returned, on average, 5.7 times the original investment!

Only a few studies explore the effectiveness of coaching by looking at effects other than coachee satisfaction. One study without a control group is that of Olivero et al. (1997), who studied 31 managers from the health care sector. The latter took part in a three-day training course, followed by eight weeks of coaching. They found that both the training and the coaching increased productivity considerably, with the bulk of the increase attributable to the coaching (average 22 per cent increase due to training and 88 per cent due to training and coaching). Ragins et al. (2000) studied a group of 1162 professionals from many organisations and looked at the effect of formal or informal mentoring relationships on a range of work and career attitudes. Of the respondents, 44 per cent had an informal mentor, 9 per cent a formal mentor as part of a mentoring programme, and 47 per cent no mentor (control group). Their results show that the crucial factor is the mentee's satisfaction with the mentoring relationship: in the absence of satisfaction, there are no demonstrable differences between professionals who are mentored and those who are not. If the satisfaction is achieved, however, the professionals clearly demonstrate more positive attitudes towards themselves (self-confidence), their work, promotion prospects, organisation and career – albeit without significant differences between formal and informal mentoring.[1]

One of the most thorough studies into the effects of 'executive coaching' was written by Smither et al. (2003). They work with a control group and base their conclusions not only on self-evaluations, but also evaluations by independent researchers and by the coachees' superiors, colleagues and staff (360° feedback). The research was conducted among 1202 senior managers in the same multinational organisation and involved 360° feedback results from two consecutive years. The researchers find a small, but significant and positive effect in the score with regard to:

1. In this study, the authors cannot rule out the possibility that professionals with more positive mentoring relationships are relatively more satisfied in general terms, and so more satisfied with themselves, their organisation and their career. As regards the differences between formal and informal mentoring programmes (in other words, between assigned and chosen mentor relationships), it is interesting that Ragins et al. (2001) can demonstrate slightly negative effects for formal mentoring programmes where the mentees are not able to choose their mentor when (1) the mentor works in the same department as the mentee and (2) female mentees are assigned to a male mentor.

- agreeing specific goals,
- asking for ideas for improvements from superiors, and
- assessments by colleagues and superiors.

Smither et al. also ask the coachees to assess the effectiveness of their own coaching experience; as in other studies, they record high scores (a good 4 on average, on a scale of 1–5 – so 'very effective' on average!). However, generally coaching appears to be primarily a 'gift' for coachees – 'It can't do any harm so it may do some good' – and the evaluations consequently turn out always high. More independent and objective research into the effectiveness of coaching records only small effects, albeit significantly positive ones.

In the small but fast-growing body of literature on coaching we found no articles exploring the question of *what sort* of coaching is effective, and which coaching approach can best be applied to which issues. If the reader wants to know more about this, the best place to look is in psychotherapy outcome research. In our view, many of the conclusions in that field can be transposed to coaching. Much properly monitored and validated research has already been conducted in psychotherapy, and researchers have investigated which variables promote effectiveness under what conditions. There are also review articles, such as those by Beutler et al. (1986, 1994), which summarise dozens of empirical studies, and publications containing overviews of many review articles, such as Roth and Fonagy (1996).

A number of disconcerting facts emerge from research into the effectiveness of psychotherapy:

- For large groups of patients, it is possible to show that 'therapy' is more effective than 'no therapy', and indeed more effective than 'placebo therapy', but the differences compared with the latter are minimal (Lambert and Bergin, 1994).
- Therapists' behaviours in the therapy sessions themselves seem to have more in common than their theoretical approaches would lead one to believe (Corsini and Wedding, 1989).
- Personal characteristics have a greater impact on the outcome of psychotherapy than technique, method or approach, so non-specific factors have a greater impact than theory- or technique-related factors (Goldfried et al., 1990).
- Some therapists are successful in every technique, others are unsuccessful in every technique (Lambert, 1989).
- Experience, education and length of supervision are poor indicators of success (Beutler et al., 1986). Indeed, inexperienced and non-professional therapists sometimes turn out to be more effective than experienced and trained colleagues (Dumont, 1991).

Similarly, it is very difficult to carry out truly comprehensive research into the effectiveness of coaching (see Patterson, 1987). The outcomes of coaching depend on the technique and personality of the coach, the issue and personality of the coachee and the objective and context of the coaching – all six of these dimensions have to be taken into account. If we carry out a taxonomy of each dimension in only 10 classifications, we would have to research $10 \times 10 \times 10 \times 10 \times 10 \times 10 = 1$ million cells, a multivariate analysis which is humanly impossible!

However, we can conjecture something about the effectiveness of coaching, which seems to be so closely connected with the personality of the coach. The following variables appear to have a positive effect on the outcome of psychotherapy:

- Empathy, respect, warmth and genuineness – the criteria emphasised by Carl Rogers (Rogers, 1957; Goldfried et al., 1990).
- Creating an attractive (!), trustworthy and expert impression, in that order (McNeal et al., 1987).
- The emotional well-being of the therapist (Beutler et al., 1986).
- The ability to let go of one's own value system and to communicate within that of the client (see Beutler et al., 1994; also Chapter 12 of this book).

What works for whom?

The question which naturally concerns us most as a coach is: what will work for this coachee? Which approach and which method can I apply in order to best help *this* coachee, with *this* problem, in *this* coaching session? Clearly, there is no obvious answer to this question, if only because:

- In principle, any approach can be applied to any coaching issue.
- Research shows that good coaches are effective coaches, relatively independently of the approach that they apply (Lambert, 1989).
- Problems are multi-layered: coachees often ask for a certain type of 'treatment' but, at a deeper level, they need something quite different (consider, for example, the coachee who seeks advice because s/he is afraid of giving him or herself advice).
- Coaches themselves have preferences and talents that fit in with one of the approaches: for example, if you as a coach are blessed with really good listening skills, why deny yourself the person-centred approach?

However, something can be said about the effectiveness of each method; moreover, there are also some research results (for example, Roth and Fonagy, 1996).[2] Most of the suggestions below are no more than conjectures,

2. In their book *What Works For Whom?*, Roth and Fonagy (1996) summarise many hundreds of quantitative research results for therapy outcome. Their classification of therapies into five main currents corresponds very closely to our own classification into four approaches: (analytic) psychodynamic

resulting from research and our own experiences as coaches and coachees. The four approaches are discussed in the order in which they have been raised previously in this book.

The directive approach

While the directive approach is the one that emerges best from quantitative research this is partly because this approach, which focuses on measurable results, simply lends itself best to research of this nature (Roth and Fonagy, 1996). Directive approaches are particularly successful in clinical cases of depression and phobias. In these areas, directive approaches are almost 'unbeatable' when compared with other approaches: coachees start to believe in the future again and work systematically on different, more effective behaviours. If we look at the directive coaching methods in this book, we can see that the GROW METHOD and the SOLUTION-FOCUSED METHOD are the easiest and quickest to apply, due to their step-by-step, coach-directed nature, and often provide a solution in short and informal coaching conversations as well.

- A step-by-step model such as the GROW METHOD can be learned quickly and easily. The coachee always takes something away from the session: (s)he brainstorms about possible approaches, lists those approaches and makes a considered decision personally. Moreover, this method helps to structure thinking, and to examine: 'What was our goal again?'
  (*Special use:*) We prefer to use the GROW METHOD when a coaching conversation becomes aimless or 'plodding'. Asking about the 'goal' and following up with a systematic exploration of subsequent steps can restore dynamism to the coaching, and a focus on results.
  (*Contra-indication:*) The GROW METHOD is not recommended where strong emotions are involved: it is a highly practical method that completely skims over emotions, and this can result in the coachee feeling completely misunderstood. This method can also reinforce unworkable solutions, because it does not even pretend to investigate the underlying 'issue behind the issue'.
- The SOLUTION-FOCUSED METHOD is suited to coachees who are anxious about the future and have lost heart somewhat. This method often increases the coachee's enthusiasm and belief in the future. Moreover, this approach encourages the coachee to draw on reserves that are already present but are hidden from or inaccessible to them.

psychotherapy; (directive) behavioural, cognitive-behavioural and interpersonal psychotherapy; (paradoxical) systemic orientations; (person-centred) supportive and experiential therapies. The fifth main current identified by Roth and Fonagy is group therapy.

(*Special use:*) This type of coaching is especially applicable where the coachee has already fretted a lot about his or her problem and accompanying difficulties, and is somewhat 'stuck' in the past and in previous, unsuccessful approaches.

(*Contra-indication:*) Some solution-focused therapy manuals classify coachees as 'visitors', 'complainers' and 'customers' (De Jong and Berg, 2001) and express a clear preference for the latter – in other words, for coachees who see themselves as part of their problem and are prepared to work on themselves (see Chapter 6). Clearly, this method is therefore less suitable for 'difficult' coachees who do not want to change and who tend to blame others, perhaps even their own coach.

The person-centred approach

The person-centred approach offers a helpful basis for any coaching. Being open to the person of the coachee is very valuable in any coaching situation. The counsellor is concerned almost exclusively with 'being open'. As in the analytic approach, the quality of person-centred counselling usually increases with increasing experience and supervision, because these refine and train listening skills. Because the counsellor adds far fewer personal interpretations to the coachee's story, the risk of the coaching breaking down due to its careless application is greatly reduced.

- Our COUNSELLING METHOD is in fact hardly a method, more a compact reminder of the main aspects of person-centred coaching.

  (*Special use:*) In our experience, the COUNSELLING METHOD is particularly applicable where there is a lack of self-confidence and assertiveness, because this method devotes constant attention to the coachee: how (s)he feels at this moment and sees his or her problems.

  (*Contra-indication:*) Where the coachee asks for or needs – and is strong enough for! – a critical 'sparring partner', who sees through excuses and highlights weaknesses, the COUNSELLING METHOD is less suitable because it is primarily supportive and uncritical.

The analytic approach

The analytic approach is the most meticulous when it comes to exploring the problem, and is exceptionally powerful in that it subjects the interaction between coach and coachee to explicit discussion. The analytic approach prides itself on being better able than other approaches to handle multi-layered problems and coachees who do not (yet) see themselves as part of their problems. There is clear evidence that psychoanalytic therapy achieves good results in cases of depression and personality disorder (Roth and Fonagy, 1996). This is perhaps the most 'thorough' coaching approach, where coach and coachee look at possible courses of action only once the current issue has been exhaustively explored. Even then, when the coachee has mapped out a course of action and wants to proceed, the coach continues to ask questions and draw attention to alternative assumptions and courses of action. As a consequence, analytic coaching is not always quick or easy to put into action.

- The ANALYTIC METHOD and ORGANISATION COACH METHOD. Like the COUNSELLING METHOD, these methods provide a sound basis for any coaching: listening properly to the problem is central, in such a way that new, previously unseen aspects of that problem come into view.
  (*Special use:*) The ANALYTIC METHOD starts where the directive approach leaves off: with coachees who have a strong emotional involvement in their own issue and do not at first (want to) acknowledge their own part in their problem, or the issues underlying their presented issue. Instead of looking only at the 'customer' in the coachee, the ANALYTIC METHOD endeavours to expose the 'visitor' or 'complainer' in the coachee.
  (*Contra-indication:*) Effective analytic coaching calls for a great deal of training and supervision to develop the sensitivity of the coach and teach him or her how to handle transference. This method is not recommended for inexperienced coaches. The analytic method is also not recommended in short-term, results-oriented coaching, and where the coachee lacks the self-confidence needed to cope with challenging interpretations.
- The LADDER METHOD is primarily a way of applying the analytic approach in less intensive or frequent coaching. The LADDER METHOD is a specific translation of analytic principles, which can thereby be applied to more specific issues.
  (*Special use:*) This method is suitable where a coachee wants to think about his or her own assumptions systematically and is prepared to subject personal plans and emotions to a critical and strict examination.
  (*Contra-indication:*) The LADDER METHOD is less suitable for non-specific issues, or where strong emotions are involved.

The paradoxical approach

This fourth approach is manipulative in nature. For that reason alone, many coaches never want to apply it in practice. The paradoxical approach does not combine well with the person-centred approach, because of the coach's lack of transparency when using the former. If coachees are stuck in a particular defence that is interfering with the coaching itself, and if the coach lacks the time or skill to analyse that defence, paradoxical coaching can be used as an alternative to the directive and analytic approaches. We ourselves use this approach only on a short-term basis and only if the coachee, in our view, is manipulating us or sending out strongly ambiguous messages. The IRONIC METHOD is used more frequently, and is easier to use, than the more radical PARADOXICAL METHOD. Although it makes sense in most cases to use a certain approach consistently, this is much less true for the paradoxical approach: we can use it once, to stir things up or to influence the coaching relationship in some way. After that, we can continue with one of the other approaches, preferably a directive approach.

- The IRONIC METHOD is particularly useful where:
  - the coachee asks for advice, but the coach does not think that advice will help much; or
  - where the coach wants to give advice, but encounters resistance in giving it.
  For example (de Haan, 1999):
  - When a price has to be paid for accepting the advice: irony continues to point to other approaches even when a particular course has already been embarked upon.
  - When advice cannot be understood at face value: irony creates an opportunity for a deeper, more integrated understanding.
  - When the advice is too painful or disappointing: irony raises no obstacles, but provides scope for other ideas.
  - When the advice repeats something that was dismissed earlier: repetition only prompts more resistance, whereas irony places the same advice in a different perspective.
  (*Special use:*) When the coachee finds it difficult to take responsibility for his or her own situation: the IRONIC METHOD places the responsibility on the coachee. When a more 'reflective approach' is required (in other words, when we want to make the other person think more) irony offers ambiguity, and thus scope for reflection.
  (*Contra-indication:*) This method is risky if the coachee lacks self-confidence, or lacks confidence in the coaching. Take care not to apply

Figure 11.2 Sometimes, after a lot of searching, we finally end up with the right coach

an ironic approach as an 'excuse'. In a situation where it is hard for a coach to give a specific piece of advice directly because (s)he fears coachee resistance, irony can be an unhelpful 'easy way' of 'saying it anyway'.

In conclusion, we recommend that coaches should:

- choose a coaching style that fits in with their own personality;
- broaden their coaching style by trying out other methods;
- continue to develop general coaching skills, such as empathy, sensitivity and dealing with resistance, by (for example) receiving coaching themselves in the form of supervision (Hawkins and Shohet, 2000) or peer consultation (de Haan, 2004).

For more information on the use of various methods, see the following chapter, where we discuss the use of more specific interventions.

Summary: choosing the right method

There is no single best method of coaching and no single method of coaching is equally effective in every situation. The sensitivity and personality of the coach, the issue and personality of the coachee, the goals of the coaching, and the context in which it is taking place are all factors that influence the effectiveness of the methods described here. What works for whom? depends not only on the problem and the coachee, but also on the objective, the context and the personality of the coach. Assumptions for correct application of the different coaching methods:

Method	When can it be used?	Recommended where there is/are	Not recommended where there is/are
GROW METHOD	Broadly applicable, even to short, specific issues	High motivation, but little idea of possible ways to move forward	Emotional issues; non-specific issues; double meanings
SOLUTION-FOCUSED METHOD	Broadly applicable, especially to practical issues	Discouragement, anxiety about the future	'Visitors' and 'complainers', i.e. those not prepared to consider their own share in the problem
COUNSELLING METHOD	Broadly applicable, especially in a longer-term coaching relationship	Lack of self-confidence or self-motivation	Need for a critical sparring partner
ANALYTIC METHOD ORGANISATION COACH METHOD	Broadly applicable, especially to multi-layered and emotional problems	'Visitors' and 'complainers'; multi-layered issues	Need to achieve quick results and find solutions; low self-confidence
LADDER METHOD	Multilayered problems, including short, specific issues	Willingness and ability to consider their own assumptions	Non-specific issues, highly emotional issues
IRONIC METHOD	Broadly applicable	Those that ask for advice; those that do not take responsibility	Low self-confidence; lack of confidence in coaching
PARADOXICAL METHOD	In the case of ambiguous, internally contradictory questions to the coach	Strongly ambiguous messages and unclear motivation for coaching	No strong and absolutely necessary reasons for using it

NB: These suggestions are merely indications and are generally not, or at most barely, substantiated by independent research.
Conclusion: be genuine and stick with an approach that suits you!

Part III
Reflection on coaching

Introduction: 'Individuality'

'Helping' conversations are generally conversations in which someone thinks *with* you, but not *for* you. Ironically, therefore, they are often conversations in which someone is deeply involved and absorbed in your story, while at the same time remaining detached, avoiding total immersion. We have all had experiences that remind us that a truly objective and independent perspective is often more valuable than input from a compassionate colleague who 'suffers with you'. As a final reflection on 'helping' conversations, this part of the book contains four chapters which are intended to help to preserve the independence of coach and coachee. This simultaneous independence and helpfulness is often a matter of setting boundaries: boundaries between the coachee and the coach, as well as boundaries between the coachee and his or her organisation, boundaries between the coach and the other facets of the coach's personal and working life, and boundaries within the coaching relationship. We hope that these chapters can help strengthen the individuality and fortitude of the coach, who knows that (s)he can fall back on:

- the anchoring of his or her work in personal skills and qualifications (Chapter 12);
- the autonomous learning process that the coachee goes through, which takes place largely outside the coaching context (Chapter 13);
- organisational structures in the context of the coachee as a support for his/her interpretations (Chapter 14); and
- the limits of internal or external coaching, which are protected by clear codes of conduct (Chapter 15).

The four chapters go together in pairs, as in Part I.

1. Chapter 12 contains a list of *skills of the coach*, ranging from values and ethics, attitude, knowledge and relational skills to specific styles and interventions.

2. Chapter 13 concerns the development of the *skills of the coachee* and so examines the coachee's learning styles, both during coaching and during his/her career more generally. Finally

we consider the limits of learning as a coachee, when referral and solutions other than coaching are indicated.

3. Chapter 14 demonstrates how difficult it is to *monitor boundaries in coaching conversations* properly, because both coach and coachee bring different aspects of their personalities with them to the coaching process, while the coachee's organisation also plays a significant role in the sessions.

4. Finally, Chapter 15 examines the *boundaries between internal and external coaching* – i.e. the pros and cons of both – and outlines ethical boundaries in the coaching relationship, in the form of 'rules of conduct' for coaching.

12
The capabilities of the coach

There is a wide range of literature on the skills of the coach. Most books and articles about coaching contain directions and practical recommendations described from the basis of a single perspective or preferred style, such as the GROW model, Rational Emotive Therapy or Transactional Analysis. In our view, there is no single best method of coaching and different coaching styles are effective in different situations. Chapter 5 contains a broad overview of four basic approaches for coaches: *insight-focused*, *coachee-focused*, *problem-focused* and *solution-focused*. The talents and personality of the coach, the issues and personality of the coachee, the goals of the coaching and the context in which it is taking place all determine the effectiveness of any approach. An experienced coach is aware of his or her own preferred approach or approaches, and is able to deviate from them if something different appears to be more effective. *Flexibility* in choosing a personal coaching approach is perhaps the most important skill a coach can have.

However, in a general sense, there are many things to be said about the attitudes and values, knowledge, methodical skills and behavioural techniques displayed by 'good' coaches. The following pages contain some suggestions regarding the skills of the coach, based on different layers of the 'coach personality'. Ideally, those different layers should fit together well and support each other, resulting in an 'integrated coach'. Our personality structure starts with a relatively stable core and moves towards a more changeable outside: from convictions, values and ethics, to attitudes, knowledge, relational skills and specific styles, and lastly, to behaviour.

The convictions and values of the coach

The convictions and values of coaches can be as diverse as those of different family backgrounds and cultures. We do often find that coaches have a high regard for personal or cultural achievements and a certain openness to convictions other than their own.

Downey (1999) challenges coaches to consider the following basic

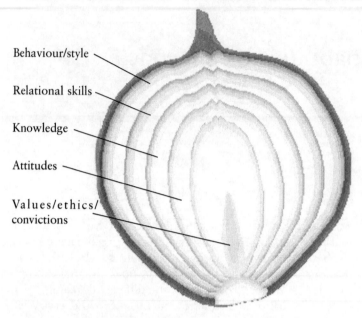

Behaviour/style

Relational skills

Knowledge

Attitudes

Values/ethics/
convictions

Figure 12.1 The coach as 'onion': structure of the personality of the coach in
five nested layers

convictions, which can underpin their effectiveness even when they are
personally in doubt about the best way forward:

- Coachees have huge potential.
- Coachees have a unique map of reality – not to be confused with reality
  itself.
- Coachees have good intentions, for themselves and for others.
- Coachees achieve their own objectives – perfectly – at all times!

Because coaching often concerns very personal problems, where one person
takes the role of client and the other the role of helper, there is a risk that the
coachee will see the coach too much as a 'leader' or 'guide' and attach excessive
importance to individual comments or signals. We have often been confronted
in our own practice with coachees who could still remember certain comments
years after the event. A good coach is well aware of the impact that coaching can
have on the coachee and weighs his or her words and gestures carefully. The
coach is continually aware that the coaching is for the coachee's benefit, not for
the greater glory of the coach, and should therefore focus exclusively on the
interests of the coachee. The coach should therefore refer the coachee elsewhere
if (s)he feels unable to help further, and has a reliable referral network of fellow
coaches and therapists. These ethical aspects of coaching are examined in more
detail in Chapter 15, where we consider codes of conduct.

Figure 12.2 The coach has many different layers, and they must all fit together properly

The attitudes of the coach

As far as we are concerned, the attitude of a coach is characterised by:

- empathy, respect, warmth and authenticity in relation to the coachee (see also Chapter 7)
- tolerance and openness to different values and opinions
- availability – calm and space for the coachee
- an appropriate balance between detachment and involvement
- an encouraging and gentle approach towards the coachee
- readiness to let the other person take initiative and responsibility
- an attitude of service towards the coachee, helping him/her to (learn how to) do it in person
- an inclination to give as little advice as possible (even if that is requested), based on the conviction that giving advice is often an insult to the other person, who has already spent a long time thinking about the issue and can give the best advice to him/herself
- a confrontational approach only if the coachee can take it and will benefit from it, otherwise a preference for supportive interventions
- humour and an ability to put things into perspective.

The knowledge of the coach

What knowledge does a good coach have? This depends partly on the coachee's question (see also Chapter 1). Where the coaching concerns questions that centre on content and specialist knowledge ('what' and 'how' questions) the coach should also have that specialist knowledge. Yet many questions asked by coachees are more personal in nature, with a link to their work ('who' questions). For example, these are questions about how the coachee holds his or her own in the organisation, how (s)he works with others or acts with respect to his or her managers. When addressing this type of question specialist knowledge is less important, and can even be an impediment (the coach might switch from coaching to giving expert advice). What knowledge, then, is relevant to addressing these 'who' questions?

- In the first place, *self-knowledge:* the coach is aware of the way in which (s)he tends to view problems, and is able to look at the coachee from multiple perspectives. The coach knows the patterns and traps lying in wait for the unwary coach (for example, being quick to give advice, asking suspicious questions, or emphasising only the positive in the coachee's account); and is aware of the emotions (s)he experiences during sessions and how to manage them professionally. The coach is also aware of his or her main qualities, which are relevant because the biggest coaching pitfalls are often associated with them.
- Good coaches have knowledge about the development of individuals and groups. They know which problems are associated with particular life stages and what patterns may emerge in them.
- Because coaching is always work-related, coaches also have knowledge about the development of organisations. This includes a sound understanding of management and change. Context-less coaching is doomed to failure (see also Chapter 14).
- Coaching is not therapy. Nevertheless, a basic knowledge of psychodynamics and psychotherapy is necessary to enable the coach to choose the right interventions, to keep a watchful eye on the boundary between coaching and psychotherapy, and to make timely referrals.
- As stated above, no single coaching style is always effective. Knowledge of different approaches to coaching, interventions and levels of intervention, as well as of your own preferred styles and interventions, is necessary in order to be able to tailor your approach to the coachee in his or her context. It is also necessary in order for you to be aware what your own contribution is at any moment in the coaching conversation.
- Coaches have extensive knowledge of communication techniques (conversational techniques, influencing styles) – in order to be effective personally in directing the conversation and to make the coachee aware of his or her effectiveness in communication and in using influence.

The strategic skills of the coach

- The coach needs a number of skills in order to mould his or her approach consistently over a longer period and so create a context for constructive interventions within coaching sessions:
- Coaches are able to engage in and maintain diverse types of *relationship*: they have the ability to build up and wind down relationships with a wide range of coachees, to create the working alliances in which coaching becomes possible. It helps in this respect to be clear, unambiguous and consistent, and to be able to tolerate a wide range of feelings, both within oneself and in others.
- An effective coach is able to use the different areas of knowledge outlined above effectively in the coaching context. This starts with *effective management of expectations*, an issue that comes up afresh in every session. The coach is transparent and checks regularly that the goals of the coaching are clear and attainable.
- An effective coach *can work consistently with different approaches* – for example, insight-focused, coachee-focused, problem-focused and solution-focused – and makes a considered choice, depending on the question, the coachee and his/her context.
- Irrespective of the approach adopted, a coach is good at *recognising patterns and mental models*. The coach is on the lookout during the sessions for possible links between the 'here and now' and the coachee's issue as presented.
- Perhaps most importantly, a coach is able to manage his or her own many painful experiences in coaching conversations, as in the case of:
  - ambiguity, 'not understanding' and 'not knowing'
  - managing his/her own emerging 'stuff', in the form of personal judgements, recollections and expectations
  - handling criticism, unrealistic expectations and transference.

Along the lines of the list of ten defences in Chapter 8, to which the coach as well as the coachee must not fall prey, the coach would do well to develop an *eleventh defence*, namely a buffer between stimulus and response – staying calm and attentive in a situation marked by painful stimuli.[1]

The specific interventions of the coach

A useful model for the different specific skills that the coach can use at any moment in a coaching conversation is provided by John Heron (1975). The six styles proposed by Heron can be represented effectively (Figure 12.3) in our 'window onto the coach' from Chapter 2.[2]

1. This strategic skill is sometimes referred to as a *negative capability* (Bion, 1970).
2. We have renamed Heron's 'six categories of counselling intervention' as follows:

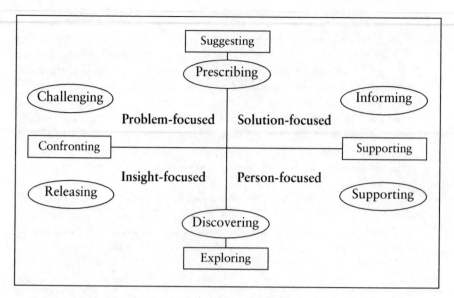

Figure 12.3 The window onto the coach: six specific behavioural styles of
coaches

Three of these styles are relatively directive (challenging, directing and
informing) and three are more facilitative (releasing, discovering, supporting). The styles can also be viewed in complementary pairs, as follows:

- *Discovering* and *directing* are both strongly directional, one from the
  coachee and the other from the coach.
- *Releasing* and *challenging* are both confrontational, although the former
  is much less critical of the coachee than the latter.
- *Supporting* and *informing* are both supportive, the former on the basis
  of feelings and the latter on the basis of content.

In the application of the different coaching approaches from Part II, it is clear
that each of those approaches relies particularly on a subset of the six styles. For
example, the COUNSELLING METHOD makes use almost exclusively of *discovering* and *supporting* – even *releasing* would shift the perspective too much
towards the coach and weaken the internal 'locus of evaluation'. Similarly,
discovering and *releasing* are the main styles for the ANALYTIC METHOD, while
directing, *informing* and *challenging* are the main styles of the PARADOXICAL
METHOD. In the SOLUTION-FOCUSED METHOD, *directing* and *informing* are the

prescriptive–directing, cathartic–releasing, confronting–challenging, supportive–
supporting, informative–informing, catalytic–discovering. We adopt Heron's definitions in terms of skills here, but their placement in the 'window onto the
coach' is ours.

main styles used by the coach, who uses a lot of *discovering* and *supporting* within those styles at a more content-related level, while the GROW METHOD can also use *challenging* in addition to those styles.

The following tables contain more detailed information on the different coaching styles. Before you read these tables in detail, it is recommended that you inquire about your own dominant coaching styles. In Appendix E we present the Coaching Behaviours Questionnaire, a tool with which to explore your own coaching styles.

Figure 12.4 Coaching can be a very enjoyable activity

Directive coaching styles

1. Directing

Specific behaviours:
- Giving directions, advice, recommendations, suggestions
- Contributing to alternatives and suggestions of the coachee
- Insisting on a specific approach
- Motivating with clear instructions

Examples of interventions:
- 'Have you also thought of …?'
- 'I think it would be good for you to …'
- 'My approach is …'
- 'I suggest …'

Traps to avoid:
- Giving unsolicited advice
- Taking over and imposing solutions
- Directing the conversation too much
- Creating dependence on the part of the coachee
- Weak application by doubting, hesitating or undermining your own advice – or by being over-controlling

When to use:
- When the coachee lacks self-confidence
- When the coachee is unable to direct own learning
- When (ethical, legal, safety, professional) guidelines are imposed

2. Informing

Specific behaviours:
- Imparting information and knowledge
- Presenting new perspectives
- Adding interpretations and summaries
- Checking understanding
- Answering questions

Examples of interventions:
- 'That book contains further information on …'
- 'To my knowledge the most important approaches are …'
- 'That seems (il-)logical, because …'
- 'My own answer to that is as follows …'

Traps to avoid:
- Overloading with information
- Too much jargon
- Too little underlying structure
- Too little linking with the directing style: unclear why information is given
- Too much emphasis on coach as 'teacher': teaching versus learning focus

When to use:
- If asked to explain something
- Adding missing information
- Describing one's own experiences
- Structuring the coachee's story

3. Challenging

Specific behaviours:
- Giving feedback
- Posing direct questions
- Testing (underlying) assumptions
- Challenging possible defences, excuses and evasions
- Encouraging (self-)reflection

Examples of interventions:
- 'That's not how you come across to me.'
- 'Do you realise that you are not making use of important talents?'
- 'I am not sure you are very clear on this.'
- 'Are you assuming that it is the same problem as last year?'
- 'One could also look at that quite differently ...'
- 'I have just heard a lot of positive things about your report.'

Traps to avoid:
- All of the traps associated with the giving of feedback[3]
- Too much emphasis on the coach as 'independent assessor'
- External 'locus of evaluation'[4]
- Putting relationship to the test over a 'trivial' matter
- Escalation to competition between coach and coachee

When to use:
- To increase the (self-)insight of the coachee
- To increase insight into perceptions of others, or into the possible consequences of actions
- To challenge the coachee to reconsider automatic assumptions
- To reinforce self-confidence by providing positive feedback

3. See also Chapter 10 of *Learning with Colleagues*.
4. See also Chapter 7 of this book.

Facilitative coaching styles

1. Discovering

Specific behaviours:
- Asking questions and listening
- Reflecting back statements or feelings of the coachee
- Paraphrasing and summarising
- Inviting new perspectives from the coachee

Examples of interventions:
- 'How would you like to start?'
- 'What do you mean by ...?'
- '...?'
- 'What advice would you offer someone else in your situation?'
- 'What do you think about it yourself?'
- 'What would you do differently?'

Traps to avoid:
- Too many questions
- Asking closed questions
- Suggestions concealed in questions
- Structuring too soon
- Being led by your own curiosity instead of that of the coachee
- Contributing your own experiences and allowing them to dominate
- Not clarifying – by asking! – the objectives

When to use:
- Good basis for *any* coaching conversation!
- To foster deeper understanding, especially in the coachee
- To help the coachee assume more responsibility
- To promote commitment, self-motivation, self-evaluation and self-confidence

2. Supporting

Specific behaviours:
- Expressing appreciation
- Displaying confidence
- Displaying availability, involvement, concern
- Explicitly increasing self-confidence
- Expressing shared feelings

Examples of interventions:
- 'You did that well'
- 'I can imagine that you're worried about that.'
- 'I'll be here again tomorrow morning if you need me'
- 'I am confident that you will make this a success'
- 'Don't worry if all of the details have not been worked out.'

Traps to avoid:
- Flattery, false compliments and exaggeration
- Against all odds: 'yes, but ...'-type support
- Exaggerated protection; patronising the coachee
- Being held back by own inhibitions

2. Supporting (cont)

- Giving mixed signals
- Levelling off using 'plusses' and 'minuses'

When to use:
- To build morale and self-confidence
- To offer support in taking risks
- As an approach to 'withdrawn' coachees
- To encourage learning from success

3. Releasing

Specific behaviours:
- Active and focused listening
- Asking follow-through questions
- Asking about what 'seems to be hard to say', or 'what is left unsaid'
- Self-disclosure, empathy and sharing own feelings
- Reflections on the coachee's feelings at this moment
- Inviting underlying and different perspectives

Examples of interventions:
- 'Why do you lack self-confidence?'
- 'What is going on here?'
- 'By the way in which you talk about it you seem to be saying ...'
- 'What exactly?'
- 'What you seem to be talking about less this time is ...'
- 'Is it difficult to talk about that here?'
- 'But you don't seem to feel confident about that.'
- 'That leaves me feeling rather lost.'

Traps to avoid:
- Filling in too much for the coachee
- Psychologising; going too deep
- Making a mountain out of a molehill
- Showing sympathy too easily
- Losing own independence by feedback or support
- Denying or criticising coachee's feelings (unintentionally)
- Putting up barriers for the coachee

When to use:
- To deepen insight
- To make space for new perspectives
- When the coachee feels blocked or incompetent
- When the coachee is frustrated, demotivated or angry
- When the coachee is afraid to take risks

Finally, we give a list of common and more elaborate coaching interventions which are not so easy to classify in terms of Heron's coaching styles:

Interventions	Matching coaching approaches	Matching coaching styles
Reflection on the coachee's use of language, e.g.: • talking without using the first person: 'you', 'people', 'everyone' • talking in terms of impossibilities • indirect allusions which may refer to this conversation or the coach, for example.	Analytic	Depending on directive or facilitative intervention: *informing* or *discovering*
Pattern recognition, such as reflection on: • links with what was said in a previous session • repetition of certain words or expressions • use of certain types of imagery and associations.	Analytic	Depending on directive or facilitative intervention: *releasing* or *challenging*
Converting objections into opportunities, e.g.: • by using the question 'How could it be done?' if the coachee keeps pointing out why something cannot be done • by the 'miracle question' (see Chapter 6).	Directive Solution-focused	Depending on directive or facilitative intervention: *directing* or *discovering*
Research in the form of questionnaires, e.g. concerning personality, stress indicators, learning styles, leadership styles, team roles etc.	Directive Analytic	Combination of *directing* (handing out questionnaires) and *discovering* (about the coachee)
Homework in the form of diary, biography, logbook, coaching conversation report, mind map, story, drawing, etc.	Directive	*Directing*
Exercises in the form of role-play with the coach or with the aid of a video camera in the workplace.	Directive	*Directing, informing* and *challenging*

Summary: the capabilities of the coach

The convictions held by different coaches can vary widely, but good coaches are transparent about them and open to alternatives.

The most important attitude is one of respect for the coachee and involvement in the coachee's learning process.

A successful coach has self-knowledge, knows his or her own style and is able to deviate from it if a different style appears to be more effective. In addition, (s)he has knowledge of:

- development of individuals and groups
- organisation and change management
- psychodynamics and psychotherapy
- approaches to coaching, interventions and levels of intervention
- communication techniques.

An effective coach is skilled at:

- maintaining relationships with a wide variety of coachees
- managing expectations
- working with different methods
- recognising patterns and mental models
- utilising painful impressions and experiences.

The behaviour of an effective coach can be characterised as focusing on the following six central coaching styles:

- directing or giving directions, advice and recommendations
- informing or giving information, knowledge and summaries
- challenging or increasing (self-)awareness and exploring assumptions
- discovering or deepening insight by facilitating self-exploration
- supporting or raising self-confidence and self-esteem
- releasing or exploring emotions which are blocking progress.

13
Learning through coaching

Coaching is a form of individual learning which helps people to progress in their professional development – their 'career'.[1] In this chapter we examine how coaching fits in with individual learning styles and individual careers. We also explore situations when coaching is perhaps not the best answer. As a coach, reflecting on the coachee's learning can help you emphasise the autonomy of the coachee and so avoid becoming too involved yourself. Finally, the role of the coach is to encourage the coachee's autonomous learning process. The coachee remains the owner of that process: (s)he will have to go through it in person!

Coaching and individual learning styles

Being coached is a very personal and completely unique experience. Mindful of Rogers' well-known words,[2] however, we can still perhaps make some general comments about this personal and unique experience. What is the impact of coaching, and how can a coach reinforce that impact? Coachees report that coaching can have an impact on many fronts – sometimes even apparently opposing ones – through (for example):

- facilitating reflection on one's day-to-day practice
- facilitating reflection on one's own role at work, and on one's own career
- providing a haven and support when going through transitions at work
- offering challenge and inspiration in breaking out of periods of stagnation at work
- helping find new answers and untapped potential

1. Earlier, in Chapter 8, we wrote about 'learning' as a possible defence for the coachee against new insight. In this chapter, we write about the opposite: learning not as a method of masking repression but as an expression of authentic progress and change.
2. 'The most personal is the most universal' – see Chapter 7.

- allowing preparation and practice of a new attitude or new behaviour at work.

Learning is personal, and different professionals differ with regard to how they would prefer to learn (see *Learning with Colleagues*, Part III). In his book *Experiential Learning* (1984), Kolb describes four different learning styles. If we think of coaching as stimulating individual learning processes, it is important for a coach to know which learning style best suits the coachee. To this end Kolb drew up the *learning style inventory*, which we included in *Learning with Colleagues* as Appendix D. Kolb identifies the following learning styles:

Divergent
In this learning style you consider specific situations from many different perspectives and establish links between different aspects and approaches. Besides listening and looking carefully, your imagination and powers of observation help you to consider events, issues or problems from a variety of angles. This is a *divergent* learning style because you keep seeing new aspects, which keep leading to new meanings and values. It is especially suited to the appropriation of new experiences and the generation of new ideas. Interest in, and sensitivity to, personal and interpersonal aspects often go hand-in-hand with this learning style.

Assimilative
In this learning style you move from diverse observations and reflections to an integrated explanation or to theoretical models. Using precision and sharp logic, you judge information and models on their merits. This is an *assimilative* learning style, because you assimilate diverse ideas and information or adapt them to an encompassing theoretical framework. This learning style is especially suited to the inclusion of data in models, and when testing whether these models are complete and offer a basis for generalisation. The learner's interest lies mainly in the beauty and completeness of the models themselves, at the expense of interest in people or in practical matters.

Convergent
In this learning style you combine theory and practice in usable and achievable solutions. Using selective attention, problem-solving capability and progress-oriented decision-making, you adapt and apply models in order to provide new answers and solutions to practical questions. This is a *convergent* learning style, because the style helps you get to grips with complex and ambiguous experiences and transform them into a single experiment or defensible approach. This learning style is therefore eminently suited to situations where a single hypothesis or solution is necessary and possible. Concentrated attention and the nerve to break new ground and take decisions often go hand-in-hand with this learning style.

Accommodative

In this learning style you can achieve practical results by rolling up your sleeves, trying things out and seeking out new experiences. Using adaptability, commitment and entrepreneurship, you take steps to follow up choices and try out solutions. This is an *accommodative* learning style, because you react and adapt to changing circumstances. It is particularly suited to complex situations in which progress is required, and where 'trial-and-error' offers a good approach. The learner's interest here is often intuitive and implicit, directed towards action, influence, mastery and new experiences.

A coach can act within each of a number of facilitative roles (compare Chapter 16 of *Learning with Colleagues*), serving as:

- a developer within divergent learning, encouraging reflection and different ways of looking at things
- a teacher within assimilative learning, encouraging reading and research, linking with theory and literature and helping to structure divergent learning
- a process manager within convergent learning, preparing and testing new approaches
- a trainer within accommodative learning, giving support, looking for opportunities to practise and encourage actual application of skills and learning
- a sparring partner between the learning styles, encouraging balance and approaches other than the usual, preferred style
- a meta-teacher between the learning styles, inviting the coachee to look at the quality of the learning itself and at his or her own way of learning (in other words, inviting meta-learning).

Coaching may therefore facilitate learning processes in all of the different learning styles. Due to its conversational nature, however, and because it occurs away from the workplace, it is geared primarily towards divergent learning, just like the 'coaches' or 'consultants' in peer consultation (see Chapter 19 of *Learning with Colleagues*).

Coaching and individual careers

If we take a longer-term perspective, then coaching is located somewhere within the coachee's 'individual career' and aims to enrich and facilitate that career by raising his or her relationship with certain experiences, ambitions and issues for discussion The extent to which the longer term – and hence the coachee's career trajectory – is a subject of coaching depends, of course, on the objective of the coaching, and differs for each unique coaching relationship. If coaching has an impact, however, it will certainly have an impact on the coachee's future career as well. This is why we also consider its effects on professional careers.

Combining the insights within influential articles by Kanter (1989) and Arthur (1994), we can assume four different generic careers or 'career scripts':

- The *bureaucratic career* entails moves from rank to rank and job to job in a succession of hierarchical positions. In this pattern, people are not particularly attached to specific tasks or colleagues, but are often very loyal to the organisation as a whole. Progress in this career is vertical – the only way is up! If progress stagnates it is usually because the person concerned does not understand the rules of the game, or does not apply them properly.
- The *entrepreneurial career* is focused on entrepreneurship. In this script, professionals are entrepreneurial, creative, innovative and competitive. Once they have found their niche, they stay there. The more commercial success, the more income. Progress in this career is strongly linked to the extent to which someone is able to create new products or services. Progress stagnates when the business is not prepared to (continue to) grow.
- The *professional career* is a career based on expertise. The person concerned acquires status and reputation by excelling in professional knowledge and skills, for example in academia. The professional is very loyal to his or her specialism, but less so to the organisation. Progress is assessed in terms of an individual's response to increasingly demanding assignments. It stagnates when the professional notices, too late, that his or her specialism is no longer necessary and fails to develop a new specialism in time.
- The *boundaryless career* has no standardised script. Professionals write their own script while working on projects – often in a self-employed capacity or in temporary networks. They create progress by continually developing new things, both in terms of form and content, and by renewing their own network. Each new project brings a new challenge. Progress in this career takes place when the person concerned feels ready to take on increasingly complex and uncertain assignments. Progress stagnates if (s)he makes choices without carefully considering his or her own interests, or lacks market discipline, resilience and/or powers of recovery.

These four types of career entail different sorts of learning issues. The following barriers can be identified:

- In the *bureaucratic career* there is a risk of passive, risk-averse learning behaviour and it is particularly difficult to develop accommodative learning.
- In the *entrepreneurial career*, the usual focus on action and objectives is at odds with the calm and reflection of divergent learning, in particular.

- In the *professional career*, there are already so many intrinsic, content challenges that these 'knowledge workers' sometimes do not take on extrinsic challenges and may have difficulty with application-oriented, convergent learning.
- In the *boundaryless career* there is a lot of experience of meta-learning, but professionals may be so exposed to fragmentation, discontinuity and an excess of information that confusion results, and systematic assimilative learning in particular becomes difficult.

Coaches can, as usual, point out what is missing and what appears to be going badly. They can help more generally by, on the one hand, helping the coachee to break out of periods of stagnation and, on the other, helping bring calm to periods of transition.[3] Professionals can go through substantial transitions, for example by acquiring new responsibilities in new jobs, new contacts with clients, and new sorts of assignments. These transitions call for new knowledge, skills and behaviour, which are themselves essential components of their learning processes. If a professional does not handle a transition well (s)he may be uncertain and unproductive for a while, and might even burn out. The dominant career thinking often associates difficulties in transitions with individuals 'not fitting in', 'not managing' or 'not being strong enough'. We prefer to describe problems of this sort as *relevant learning opportunities* that call, above all, for solid coaching.

Limits on coaching

So far we have considered a range of indicators for coaching and a variety of individual learning styles and careers to which coaches, in our view, can make a useful contribution. However, when is coaching not the right answer? When would it be sensible to initiate a different learning activity or to refer the coachee to others? We believe that the limits of effective coaching have been reached in any situation where one of the following three statements applies.

The coachee presents puzzles instead of problems

The difference between *puzzles* and *problems* is that puzzles have a single, optimal solution that can be found with the right expertise, while problems have many solutions, but are never really completely resolved. A work-related problem that the coachee can solve using the Internet, or by looking up certain information inside the organisation is, in our view, not 'interesting' enough to bring to a coach. In more general terms it is useful, in the case of 'one-off' coaching issues, to consider whether coaching is necessarily the best answer or if it would be better just to call in an expert, as in the example below.

3. Similar to the *confronting* of 'what could be done differently' versus the *supporting* of 'what is going well' in our 'window onto the coach' (Chapter 2).

An example
A director of a small charity has placed an advertisement for an office manager, who will be only the third full-time employee of the organisation. He realises that this is an important expansion of the team and that he himself has little experience of taking on staff. He therefore asks his coach to coach him in the recruitment and hiring of staff. The coach suggests that he attend a number of job interviews himself, instead of focusing on the way in which the director handles this issue during coaching conversations. This is what happens and the outcome is to everyone's satisfaction.

The coachee presents organisational rather than personal problems

Coaching, in the first instance, looks at the coachee's own stake in a problem, and the way in which (s)he can strengthen and develop his or her personal contribution towards its resolution. Where organisational problems or 'team problems' are concerned, therefore, it is debatable whether coaching is appropriate. Coaching can certainly reinforce individuals in their handling of team and organisational issues, and so reinforce individuals' effectiveness in teams, but it can also reinforce a mistaken belief within an organisation that an individual coachee plays a key role in a problem of some kind. Coaching can therefore reinforce an 'individualising' tendency in the organisation, and

Figure 13.1 Sometimes the advice to enter into coaching is not the best advice

may (unintentionally) aggravate problems if it feeds a habit of placing too much emphasis on the individual's contribution to wider problems and to their resolution. In the following chapter we look in more detail at the role of the organisation in coaching issues. When considering issues involving the dynamic between groups of colleagues, *Learning with Colleagues* (de Haan, 2004) is usually a more appropriate source of information. In the case of organisational issues, it sometimes helps to call in an external organisational development consultant to look at the broader organisational system, and to work in a learning manner with the organisation as a whole.

The coachee presents all-pervading problems, extending far beyond work-related issues

If the issues for which the coachee is seeking coaching extend over many areas of his or her working and private life, coaching may not provide the right answer. If the problem is of all-pervading personal significance, and so has a constant hold on the coachee, it is important to refer him or her to a physician and psychotherapist. There are several indicators that such an all-pervading problem might be present, such as:

- disturbances and major exaggerations in the coachee's self-image or images of others
- major anxiety, expressed as anxious, attacking or controlling reactions
- insensitivity, alienation or strongly dependent behaviour.

An important indicator when deciding if coaching is appropriate is the coachee's resilience. Is the coachee able to undergo and use the sometimes painful learning experiences in the coaching?

Often, the coach realises soon enough that there is something 'fishy' going on, or that the coaching is not working. At such times it is a good idea to make a referral, to summarise your own impressions objectively and decisively, and to have recourse to names and telephone numbers of other professionals who may be able to help.

Summary: learning through coaching

Coaching is a form of individual learning in which coachees explore their own relationship with issues in their professional development - in other words, addressing specific concerns but also with regard to the broader context of their 'career'.

Kolb (1984) identifies the following learning styles:

- divergent (concrete experience)
- assimilative (reflective observation)
- convergent (abstract conceptualisation)
- accommodative (active experimentation)

Different sorts of careers may benefit from emphasising different sorts of learning issues:

- the 'bureaucratic' career, in which accommodation in particular is difficult
- the 'entrepreneurial' career, in which divergence in particular is difficult
- the 'professional' career, in which convergence in particular is difficult
- the 'boundaryless' career, in which assimilation in particular is difficult.

The coach can support the coachee in tackling these learning issues, offering assistance in going though and balancing periods of stagnation and transition in career development.

Sometimes coaching is not the right answer to an individual problem, for example:

- when dealing with puzzles instead of problems
- when an issue is more truly an organisational than an individual one
- when severe or complex personal issues on the part of the coachee are in play.

14
The organisation coach

Every coach is an organisation coach. All coaching described in this book is coaching not only of a coachee, but also of an organisation, because the coachee's organisation is present in and through every coachee. This is the main difference between coaching and psychotherapy: coaching is work- and organisation-oriented, while therapy is more remote from the working organisation – the organisation being only one dominant system of which the coachee forms part.

This chapter is concerned with the 'use' of the organisation in coaching conversations. It therefore focuses on external coaching slightly more than other chapters. We assume that the coach here is not part of the coachee's organisation. However, internal coaches can also find something for themselves here: the word 'organisation' is a broad and vague concept. For example, if the coach is part of a corporate services department and the coachee's position is deep within a division or business unit, we can safely assume that the coach is not part of the coachee's relevant organisation. The coach is therefore 'external' enough to apply the principles outlined in this chapter. For the limitations of internal coaching, see also Chapter 15.

This chapter looks primarily at the struggles, shortcomings and conflicts within the coach/coachee and coach/coachee/organisation relationships. We therefore concentrate to some extent on negative or imperfect aspects of organisation coaching. However, in our view the positive and constructive thing about coaching is precisely that the coach can draw attention to, examine and perhaps resolve these aspects. We provide only brief descriptions of the different ways of looking at the dynamics of the coach/coachee/organisation triad, but references to relevant literature are also given.

The psychodynamics of organisations

We cannot cover the whole of the theory of organisation in this book, of course – not even what has been said about it from a psychodynamic perspective – but we can raise some relevant aspects regarding working in an organisational context and discuss how those aspects can come into play in coaching conversations.

We are all members of different groups and organisations, and we all have some degree of ambivalence about working and living in groups. In short, groups are hard to live with, but also hard to live without. We have great difficulty in giving up parts of our individuality in order to fit into an organisation yet we find it hard, if not impossible, to live or work without connections. For the sake of convenience, we view organisations here in terms of activities of sensemaking (Weick, 1995) and adjustment (De Board, 1978) with regard to a variety of processes and activities. In *Learning with Colleagues* (Chapter 22), the following three, fairly general, processes in organisations were distinguished:

- *Working*, which includes the primary process of the organisation, but also a variety of jobs and tasks that employees take on for various reasons.
- *Controlling* or *managing*, which includes the management of the organisation, but also a range of local management tasks such as the development of a departmental strategy, annual departmental plans, a planning and control cycle, meetings, daily planning, and so on.
- *Learning:* all efforts to acquire knowledge in order to bring about improvements in the other two processes.

All members of organisations have to keep defining and re-defining their own positions in relation to these 'organising processes', *via* sensemaking and adjustment. Most coaching conversations concern doing this as effectively as possible: in other words, they concern boundaries, authority and taking responsibility (Czander, 1993). Coaching is about *boundaries to*, *authority within*, and *responsibility for* the role adopted by the coachee in the organisation.

Often, the aim of a professional within an organisation is to connect his or her own thoughts and feelings to processes that are of personal relevance, in the form of *role behaviour*. Role behaviour means the ability (Reed, 2000):

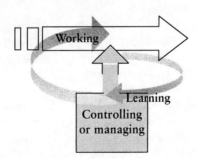

Figure 14.1 Working, managing and learning processes in organisations

- to find a role (finding a suitable work process or function; analysing the state of that process)
- to make a role (flexibility and authority in creating a suitable role)
- to take a role (assuming responsibility for and authority within one's own role).

Right from the start of coaching, it is important to think in terms of roles. If we simply look at the coachee's issue and disregard the coachee's organisation, we initially ask ourselves the question: 'Why is this dysfunctional?' If we consider the issue from the perspective of the psychodynamics of organisations, however, we ask ourselves the completely different question: 'Why is this issue thought to be dysfunctional?' We follow up with another question: 'And how does this issue, which may have a negative significance for the coachee in his or her own environment, impinge upon the functioning of the greater whole?'

As the coach, it is therefore helpful to ask yourself regularly during coaching conversations: 'How does this problem contribute to the functioning of a greater whole? What is the function of this problem? Why did it arise, and what role does it play in the continuation of the *status quo*?'

The coach in the role of coach

The coaching conversation, too, involves two clearly different roles, to which the two parties adjust to a greater or lesser extent: the role of coach and the role of coachee. In the previous chapters we discussed many characteristics of – and hence boundaries to – the role of coach. See, for example, Chapter 12 on the coach's capabilities, or the role choices in the different approaches in Part II. Many of the boundaries concern the coach's availability to focus on the coachee and the 'material' of the coachee:

- As the coach, you confine yourself largely to observation and exploration: seeing and saying what you see.
- As the coach, you dissociate yourself as far as possible from your own memory and desires (Bion, 1970), in order to be present here and now in this situation as far as possible.
- As the coach, you also have a 'negative' capability (Bion, 1970): the ability to be in situations where uncertainty, ambiguity and doubt prevail, without making laborious attempts to get out of them, for example by means of observations, interpretations and solutions.

Perception has its own limitations and is subject to distortion. In fact, much of perception is a magnificent *illusion* that we conjure up ourselves (de Haan, 1994). Yet illusions, while they subtly deceive us, also frequently enable us to explore our surroundings better. It is these illusions that enable us to take in the 'right' information. Consider a television set. If we were to see it as it is – as a distorted, multi-coloured, changing series of flat images – we could no longer take in the content of the programmes. Illusions come about by *filtering and aggregating*, removing from our consciousness the unimaginable amount of information that is available to us but that we do not need in order to act. Illusions are the result of collecting the 'raw' information on a higher aggregation level. Whether or not illusions are a by-product of that process is a question that remains unanswered. Perhaps it is precisely *thanks to* our illusions that we can use our perceptions in order to act! Illusions often relate, therefore, to our own generalisations, and to the things that we ourselves 'take for granted'.

Selective attention also contributes to a distorted view of reality and enables us to expand our scope for action and, more importantly, to choose what we want to perceive.

Finally, there are the *distortions*: the things that we do not see or see poorly because we have not developed any sensitivity to them, or because we have (often unconsciously) developed barriers or prejudices against them as a result of our own experience.

The aspects of perception outlined above are difficult to apply in coaching because they would no longer be illusions, selections or distortions if we were fully aware of them. They would become different perspectives, ways of looking at things that we could use as we choose. Especially when confronted with confusion and ambiguity, we often feel we do not have control over our perceptions, and feel ourselves inadequate. We then sometimes feel frustrated and think that we need more information, more perceptions. However, we may be deceiving ourselves by our own – not entirely conscious – realisation that more accurate perception might give rise to all sorts of painful feelings. The art is sometimes to convert 'not being able to perceive' into 'perceiving what is not there': something that is missing, that does not fit in, that is incongruous ...

It is therefore helpful, as the coach, to ask yourself regularly during coaching conversations: 'What am I not perceiving?' What is missing from the coachee's story? What aspects of the story do I find hard to make sense of? What 'colour' are my own (metaphorical) glasses at this moment? It is difficult but, with training, not impossible, to perceive one's own 'perspective', or way of perceiving!

The coachee in the role of coachee

The tensions in the coachee – in terms of 'being' coachee – have already been discussed, in Chapters 8 and 9 among others.

Coachees frequently come to the coach not in order to change, but as a last resort in order to stay the same. Consequently, the initial question is often at best a symptom of an underlying question that the coachee is initially unable or afraid to raise.[1] The initial question then acts to divert attention away from,

---

1.   The original Greek word *symptoma* means literally 'accident' or 'discomfort'.

and to hide, the actual problem. It is difficult to underestimate how painful change is, or the lengths to which coachees and organisations will go in order to avoid it. They often prefer to live with a 'symptom': a painful inconvenience that simply will not go away, and over which they have limited influence. The coachee's initial question often translates as: 'Help me without taking my symptom away'; or 'Just take my symptom away and don't change anything else'; or 'Change me without changing me!'

The coach's basic principle is generally: 'In order to change you will have to learn.' However, 'learning' can also be used to avoid change: it can act as a last line of defence (see the list of defences in Chapter 8) for the coachee. Learning is not the same as 'becoming' or 'growing'. Learning can mean understanding what is going on and leaving it at that. Learning can easily become a goal in itself.

If the issue is worth the trouble of entering into a coaching relationship, there are usually powerful emotions at stake. These emotions will be connected with the issue, the problem and failed attempts to resolve it to date, but also with entering into the coaching relationship itself. The latter feelings occur both in the coachee and in the coach.

Much of the emotional charge of a coaching relationship, especially at the start (see also Chapter 4), is still unprocessed and so is partly unconscious. Unprocessed emotional charge can be expressed in a variety of ways: resisting behaviour, controlling behaviour, attributions to others in the form of projections, and so on.

For the coachee, coaching is a process which begins with a cocktail of emotions, and moves first towards contemplation of those emotions and then to action – instead of acting immediately on the basis of those emotions. This process can be seen as the transformation of emotional experience into new opportunities for action (see Bion, 1965). 'Acting' in this context means making use of the thinking – not in the first instance to learn, but rather to become and to grow.

It is therefore helpful, as the coach, regularly to ask yourself: 'How does this coachee want me to feel?' In other words: what impact does my coachee's story have on me? What aspect of the story do I find hard to make out? How does it feel to be in conversation with the coachee at this moment?

The coachee in the role of coachee and of professional in the organisation

The coachee is the person who translates and applies the outcome of coaching conversations in his or her own practice. With the aid of coaching, (s)he makes renewed sense of the situation, and prepares to adapt accordingly. The coachee is the link between the coaching relationship and organisational practice. In fact, for the coachee, entering into a relationship with a coach means an additional adjustment and finding a new role, namely that of coachee of this coach. Because it is a role that is situated partly outside of his or her ordinary working

practice, it offers greater opportunities for gaining insight and for experiment-
ing. However, it is sometimes useful to look at your coachee as a *translator* or
intermediary between coach and organisation. This is particularly true if it
emerges that certain actions planned during the coaching conversation are not
carried out in the coachee's refractory day-to-day practice – in other words,
when the coachee experiences (in the view of the coach) a 'relapse'.

The coachee attempts to develop within a role provided by his or her
organisation. The coachee develops him/herself and a personal role at the
same time. On the basis of life experience, the coachee brings along all sorts
of (behavioural) patterns, which are visible in his or her role-behaviour. After
some time in the role, moreover, the coachee carries the organisation inter-
nally, as in a hologram.[2] A hologram has the amazing property that a fragment still contains the entire original image. Like a hologram, the coachee
reflects elements of his or her entire emotional experience in an organisation
in every fragment of conversation. Like a fragment of the hologram, the
coachee presents a complete and personal image of the organisation. The
coachee's problems and emotions can often be related to the problems and
emotions prevailing within the organisation. It is as if the organisation is
contained within the coachee, just as the coachee is contained within the
organisation. Coaching may start from either angle.

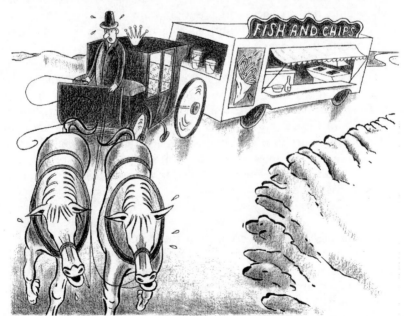

Figure 14.2 The coachee's entire organisation is present during a coaching
          conversation

2. This phenomenon of representing in oneself the emotional experience within the
    organisation is also known as the 'organisation in the mind' (see Armstrong, 1997).

It is possible to carry out a *role analysis:* in other words, to explore with the coachee his or her available roles, and the choice of roles that may be open (Reed, 2000). The following distinctions can be made in this respect:

- *Role biography* focused on the coachee: what roles has the coachee played in this and in other work processes, and what experiences are associated with those roles?
- *Role history* focused on the organisation: what roles has the organisation traditionally offered and nurtured?
- *Role dialogue* focused on both: what conversation or negotiation takes place – partly unconsciously – between organisation and coachee, in order to arrive at the most appropriate role interpretation?

Pay attention during the coaching to the coachee within yourself: be aware of what the coachee and what (*via* the coachee) the organisation triggers in you.[3] This can tell you a great deal about the less conscious aspects of the organisation in the experience of the coachee. Pay attention too to the coach within yourself. What needs, unprocessed emotions, uncertainties, change issues and other factors do you bring to this coaching relationship yourself?

Why did you actually choose the role of coach in the first place?

It is helpful, as coach, to ask yourself regularly during coaching conversations: 'How does this coachee's organisation want me to feel?' In other words, what sort of function do I fulfil as a coach in the coachee's organisation? For what stories and emotions am I a 'safety valve'?

This question can also be put to the coachee: 'How does your organisation want you to feel?' What is the emotional 'value' of your role in the organisation? What is it that you are taking on for this organisation, as a coachee? This may put you on the track of phenomena known as *valencies* (see Bion, 1961, or *Learning with Colleagues*, Chapter 12): susceptibilities of certain people and roles in organisations to particular emotional charges, which express themselves most – or even exclusively – in that person and role. Valency can therefore relate to an individual susceptibility, but also to a susceptibility associated with a certain role in the organisation.

An example

There is a preliminary meeting with the coachee, the director of a consultancy, and his manager, the majority shareholder in the consultancy. Strikingly, the coachee asks the coach for 'positive support' and 'a constructive approach' and even warns of the risk of 'burnout'.

In the first coaching conversation a few weeks later, the coachee says how ridiculously hard he has worked in recent years and how he

---

3. Compare the utilisation of *counter-transference* as described in Chapter 8. See also the *organisation coach step* in the ANALYTIC METHOD in Chapter 10.

is not accustomed to complaining about it: 'I don't know where my limits lie.' The image of 'burning' recurs, now in the form of 'fire-fighting'. This is his most frequent activity at work, but a change has occurred: recently he has been confronted on a daily basis with his own limitations and with failure.

He talks a lot about the majority shareholder, whom he experiences as negative, undermining and intimidating. He himself realises how, after his last promotion, the shareholder started to see him as a threat for the first time. In recent months he has therefore combined the valencies of 'protegee' and 'scapegoat' and it is starting to become too much for him. The coach feels paternal, concerned, caring. It is as if he is being called on to supply all of the behaviour not shown by the majority shareholder and the other consultants in the firm ...

Figure 14.3 The coach and coachee

Behind the coach stands the emotional experience of the coach, who is sensitive to what the coachee triggers in him or her. Behind that are the reserves of the coach: other aspects of his or her personality that may be brought to this coaching conversation.

Behind the coachee stands the organisation in the emotional experience of the coachee, traces of the coachee in his or her role in the organisation. Behind that are the reserves of the coachee, other roles, life experiences, that are present both in that role, and in this coaching conversation

Summary: the organisation coach

Every coach is an organisation coach: the coachee's organisation is just as present as the coachee personally. The coachee continues to be part of the organisation and the coachee has built up an internal representation of the organisation of which (s)he is part, so all coaching is organisation coaching.

Questions to ask yourself regularly as a coach:

- How does the coachee's (negative) problem contribute towards the (positive) functioning of the coachee or the (positive) functioning of the coachee's organisation?
- What am I seeing here and now? But also – what am I not seeing here and now?
- How does this coachee want me to feel?
- How does the coachee's organisation want the coachee to feel?
- How does the coachee's organisation want me to feel?

Struggles of the coach in the role of coach:

- influences based on his/her own memory and desires
- distorted perception due to illusions – filtering and generalisations
- distorted perception due to selective attention – his or her own interest, concentration and choices
- distorted perception due to distortions – distorting glasses and blind spots.

Struggles of the coachee in the role of coachee:

- emotions, including those connected with entering into the coaching relationship
- attachment to symptoms
- symptoms masking problems
- defences
- resistance.

Struggles of the coachee in the role of professional in his or her organisation:

- finding a role
- making a role
- taking a role
- valencies for emotions related to his/her own role.

15
Limitations of coaching
with colleagues

Coaching with colleagues is a broad concept. As discussed earlier in this book, both colleagues from outside the organisation (external coaches) and colleagues from within the coachee's organisation (internal coaches) can play a role in this respect. There are also managers who use a coaching style of management but at the same time remain hierarchically responsible for their staff, with inevitable consequences in terms of what can and cannot be discussed during a coaching session. This book is not concerned with coaching leadership, though we find that leaders are able to use most coaching styles very effectively. In the relationship between manager and 'coachee', the coachee cannot really be at the centre: the manager's task is to represent the interests of the organisation and the department, and those interests do not always coincide with the interests of the coachee.

In recent decades the perception of coaching within organisations has changed radically (Frisch, 2001). The negative status and stigma that previously attached to managers who needed a coach to support their professional development appear to have been replaced by a particularly positive status – the manager is apparently important enough to the organisation to warrant the investment in coaching. At the same time, coaching within organisations is being viewed less as a way to put derailed career paths back on track, and more as an investment in future careers. These developments have been accompanied by the phenomenon of internal coaches, which has developed into a formal staff discipline in a growing number of large organisations.

In this chapter we examine characteristics of internal coaches; the advantages and limitations of working with internal or external coaches; the application of the various styles by internal coaches; and the framework and codes of conduct, ethics and practice which we consider important in that respect.

Characteristics of internal coaches

Internal coaches differ from coaches coming from outside the organisation in two respects (Twijnstra and Keuning, 1988):

- First, the internal coach is not truly independent with respect to the organisation. The coach has a personal role to play in it, and also has his or her own (emotional) experience of the organisation. This sometimes makes it difficult for the coach to 'empty his/her mind' and listen with complete objectivity to what the coachee is saying.
- Second, the internal coach has more knowledge of the organisation and therefore a clear idea of the context within which the coachee is operating. This can be an important advantage over some external coaches who are unable to assess that context properly, with possible adverse consequences. However, it can also impede a fresh and independent assessment of the organisational context (see Chapter 14).

There are several reasons why an organisation might choose to work with internal coaches. Those reasons may derive from convictions within the organisation regarding how people should be managed. For example:

- The organisation sees coaching as an effective form of learning and wants to acquire relevant knowledge and experience of it, to enable the organisation to gain maximum benefit.
- The organisation sees regular coaching of staff as relevant to the effectiveness of the organisation and therefore wants to invest in it.

But there may also be entirely practical reasons for working with internal coaches. For example:

- The organisation wants to have constant access to coaching expertise and not to be dependent on outsiders.
- The organisation wants to keep the costs of coaching under control or offer it to broader target groups: external coaches may charge high fees.

Internal coaching can take a variety of forms. Some organisations decide to ask senior professionals to take on the role of coach on an occasional basis, in addition to their other responsibilities. This often occurs within consultancies. Other organisations decide to work with internal coaches who take on that role for the entire organisation, or they may even assemble a 'pool' of internal coaches.

Advantages of internal coaches

There are a number of advantages to working with internal coaches:[1]

- The internal coach has wide knowledge of the organisation, the sector and sometimes the coachee's discipline. This gives the coach an idea of

1. We refer to Frisch's article (2001) about internal coaches and also use the advantages of working with internal consultants mentioned by Twijnstra and Keuning (1988).

the context within which the coachee is operating and enables him or her to make progress more quickly, especially in the early stages.

- The internal coach knows something about the power relationships, culture and problems within the organisation. This sometimes gives the coachee a sense of safety and confidence.
- For coachees, the psychological barrier separating them from an internal coach is often lower. The advantage in terms of cost may play a role in this respect, but also the greater familiarity and proximity.
- The internal coach can often be contacted quickly and easily. It is easier to pop in to visit, if necessary, than it is with an external coach.
- The internal coach has more opportunity to observe what the coachee does in the organisation and can bring those observations to the coaching conversations.
- Working with internal coaches means working towards a more 'learning organisation' (Senge et al., 1994), if only because then internal professionals are more explicitly involved with their colleagues' learning.

Limitations of internal coaches – advantages of external coaches

Besides the advantages, the use of internal coaches also has a number of limitations.[2] Of course, these are also advantages in external coaching.

1. The internal coach is less free with respect to the coachee's organisation:
   - The internal coach's knowledge of an organisation can also result in a 'corporate blind spot' which prevents him or her from seeing certain (power) patterns and mechanisms, or from raising them for discussion.
   - The internal coach has a personal history within the organisation. As a result, (s)he may be more tempted to become unhelpfully directive, as in: 'what was good for the coach is good for the coachee'.
   - The internal coach is dependent upon the organisation – being on the payroll personally, (s)he has managers and is part of the system within which the coachee is operating. This can be experienced as very limiting and less confidential, both by the coach and by the coachee.
   - The internal coach often has a reputation with the coachee already, which can sometimes get in the way of the coaching.[3]

2. Again, see Twijnstra and Keuning (1988) and Frisch (2001).
3. Sue-Chan and Latham (2004) compare internal and external coaches with a wide difference in reputation in terms of (perceived) expertise and credibility. The outcome study was performed among MBA students and compared the performances of these students under three conditions: tutors as coaches, peers as coaches, and 'self-coaching' (with instructions). The internal coaches score much lower than the external coaches, and sometimes even lower than 'self-coaching'.

- The internal coach may be contractually committed to management objectives, and see the senior management of the organisation as his or her first and most important client. Just as in coaching leadership, this means that the coach cannot truly serve the coachee. We do not recommend such a contract for coaching, but realise that it is sometimes unavoidable for coaches operating from within the Human Resources function.
- The internal coach may be prone to choose an approach that is customary within the organisation (for example, solution-focused coaching in a solution-focused culture), while the coachee would sometimes be better served by a completely different approach: perhaps a person-centred approach, for example.
- Internal coaching can raise internal costs, such as administration, training, use of office space, and so on.

2. The internal coach has a less clear and well-defined relationship to the coachee:
    - Because the internal coach is part of the hierarchy, it is sometimes unclear who his or her client is for the coaching. It it his/her own boss, the coachee's boss or the coachee personally? To whom is the coach accountable, and for what? What happens, for example, if a valued coachee, after a successful coaching journey, decides on the basis of this work to leave the organisation?
    - The internal coach often quickly develops an informal, 'amicable' relationship with the coachee. Limits on the coaching conversations, and on containment of the coaching within the sessions (see Chapter 8), may suffer as a result. A temptation may arise to carry on coaching conversations 'as you go along', neglecting the monitoring of start and finish times and the importance of avoiding disruptive interruptions.

Limitations of external coaches

Every new coaching issue raises the question of whether the coachee would be better served by an internal or an external coach. The summary of advantages and limitations above may help this decision. The question should also be considered carefully before adopting one of the coaching approaches mentioned. On the basis of our own experience, as both internal and external coaches, we consider that every approach can, in principle, be applied by internal and external coaches. We do believe that some specific coaching approaches may be appropriate in particular contexts, however, remembering the fact that physical distances between an internal coach and coachee are often relatively small (especially in smaller organisations), and also the type of issues that are often brought to internal coaches. Not surprisingly, we have concluded that the directive approaches are often more suitable for internal coaching than the person-centred and analytic approaches. The latter in particular call for a proper contract, a high level of confidentiality, a clear framework and an adequate time frame.

The profession of 'coach' is perhaps one of the most unregulated professions in current business practice. There are (as yet) no universally accredited training programmes, no generally recognised codes of conduct, and no generally recognised professional associations or disciplinary boards. It is hard to say anything definite about the background and professionalism of external coaches. We do note that external coaches often have a background in psychotherapy, external management consultancy or management – or a combination of the three. Each background and each individual brings with them their own qualities and limitations as coaches. As pointed out already (see, for example, Chapter 11), other factors that come into play include the person of the coachee, the nature of the coaching issues, the type of coaching relationship that develops, and the objectives and context of coaching. What we have noticed is that:

- Coaching *management consultants* are often troubled by the possible presence of psychological health issues and problematic personal circumstances when dealing with coachees; they are generally aware of the need to have criteria for referral (see, for example, our suggestions in Chapter 13) and to build up a network among psychotherapists.
- Coaching *psychotherapists* often have trouble with the organisational context, and with both the organisation's impact on the coaching and the coaching's impact on the organisation. They tend to overlook the context to some extent and focus primarily on the thinking, feelings and actions of the individual coachee.
- Coaching *managers* often find it difficult to create the right coaching relationship, in terms of providing service and advice. They sometimes find it hard to put the coachee and his/her issues truly at the centre and to intervene in a way that respects the autonomy of the coachee.

Beyond these three fairly general comments, we find it difficult to make any broad statements about the limitations of external coaching, if only due to the great diversity of that professional field. It would be a step forward if more generally accepted qualifications and professional codes were developed in the coming years. Until then, we can only continue to emphasise how important it is that coaching should go hand-in-hand with an excellent understanding between coach and coachee, and a clear and explicit coaching contract.

Ashridge's Code of Conduct for coaches

One of the risks of internal coaching is that it is fitted in amongst normal day-to-day activities, and that internal coaches may overlook a number of rules of conduct that external professional coaches tend to adopt more explicitly. Many different codes of conduct for coaches are in use. We have based the Ashridge Code of Conduct for Coaches on the standards for professional conduct of the British Association of Counselling Practitioners (BACP) and on the ethical codes of the Dutch organisation of professional coaches (NOBCO) and of the International Coach Federation (ICF). We believe this provides a framework which is relevant to both internal and external coaches. These documents are available for reference on the Internet (see www.bacp.org.uk, www.nobco.nl and www.coachfederation.org).

The purpose of this Code of Conduct is to establish and maintain standards for coaches and to inform and protect members of the public, their individual clients and organisations seeking their services.

Ethical standards embody such values as integrity, competence, confidentiality and responsibility. Ashridge coaches, in assenting to this Code, accept their responsibility to clients, colleagues and Ashridge. The client's interest is paramount, but where coaches sense a conflict of responsibilities they have to use their considered judgement. Therefore the Code of Conduct is a framework within which to work rather than a set of instructions.

Figure 15.1 Sometimes it is difficult to open yourself up as a coach. Practical experience and knowledge, however useful, can form an obstacle to effectiveness!

General principles

Firstly, we maintain that:

1. Coach and client enter into an equal relationship which is used intentionally for the benefit of the client.
2. Clients ultimately know best what is best for them and can decide for themselves what they do or do not want, both in their private and in their professional lives; clients are therefore also responsible for the choices that they make and accountable for their actions.
3. The responsibility of the coach is to give the client an opportunity to explore, discover and clarify ways of living and working more satisfyingly and resourcefully.
4. During coaching the goals, resources and choices of the client have priority over those of the coach.

Code of ethics

ISSUES OF RESPONSIBILITY

- Coaches are responsible for observing the principles embodied in this Code of Conduct.
- Coaches accept responsibility for encouraging and facilitating the self-development of the client within the client's own network of relationships.
- The coach takes account of the developmental level, abilities and needs of the client.
- The coach is aware of his/her own cultural identity and that of the client and of the possible implications of any similarities and differences for the coaching.
- Coaches are responsible for ensuring that they are not dependent upon relationships with their clients for satisfying their own emotional and other needs.
- During coaching the coach will not engage in non-coaching relationships, such as friendship, business or sexual relationships with coachees. Coaches are responsible for setting and monitoring the boundaries between working and other relationships, and for making the boundaries as explicit as possible to the client.
- The coach will cooperate in the handling of a complaints procedure if one is brought against him/her, and makes sure that reasonable arrangements have been made for professional liability.

ISSUES OF COMPETENCE

- Coaches recognise the power inherent in their position: they realise that they can exert considerable influence, both consciously and unconsciously, on their clients and possibly also on third parties.

- Coaches are aware of the limitations both of their coaching and their personal skills and take care not to exceed either. They refer a client to a colleague, if necessary, and maintain a professional network to that end.
- Coaches commit themselves to training in coaching and undertake further training at intervals during their careers.
- Coaches seek ways of increasing their professional development and self-awareness.
- Coaches monitor their coaching work through regular supervision by professionally competent supervisors, and are able to account to individual clients, colleagues and client organisations for what they do and why.
- Coaches monitor the limits of their own competence.
- Coaches, along with their employers and organisation clients, have a responsibility to themselves and their clients to maintain their own effectiveness, resilience and ability to help clients. They must be able to identify any situation in which their personal resources have become depleted to the extent that they must seek help and/or withdraw from coaching, whether temporarily or permanently.

Code of Practice

This Code of Practice is intended to provide more specific information and guidance in the implementation of the principles embodied in the Code of Ethics.

MANAGEMENT OF THE WORK

- Coaches should inform clients as appropriate about their training and qualifications, and the methods they use.
- Coaches should clarify with clients the number and duration of sessions and fees. They should also explore a client's own expectations of what is involved in coaching with him/her.
- Coaches should gain the client's permission before conferring with other people about the client.
- Coaches should abstain from using any of the information that they have obtained during coaching for their own personal gain or benefit, except in the context of their own development as a coach.
- If there is another internal client (e.g. a manager), coaches must ensure before the coaching starts that all parties have the same information concerning the goal and structure of the coaching and the intended working method. The coaching can progress only if there is agreement between them with respect to its goals and structure. If there is any change in the situation or the assignment, the coach formally revises the arrangements with all parties.
- Coaches who become aware of a conflict between their obligations to a client and their obligation to an organisation employing them

will make explicit the nature of the loyalties and responsibilities involved.

- In situations where coaches have a difference of opinion with the client or other involved parties, they will maintain a reasonable attitude and keep dialogue open.
- Coaches work with clients to terminate coaching when the clients have received the help they sought, or when it is apparent that coaching is no longer helping them.

CONFIDENTIALITY

- Coaches regard all information concerning the client – received directly, indirectly or from any other source – as confidential. They protect their clients against use of personal information, and against its publication unless this is authorised by the client or required by law.
- Treating information 'in confidence' means not revealing it to any other person or through any public medium, except to those to whom coaches owe accountability for coaching work, or on whom coaches rely for support and supervision.
- If coaches believe that a client could cause danger to others, they will advise the client that they may break confidentiality and take appropriate action to warn individuals or the authorities.
- The coach obtains the agreement of the client before releasing his/her name, or any other client identifying information, in references – for example, for potential clients.

ADVERTISING/PUBLIC STATEMENTS

- Coaches do not advertise or display an affiliation with an organisation in a manner that falsely implies the sponsorship or verification by that organisation.
- Coaches do not make false, exaggerated or unfounded claims about what coaching will achieve.

Summary: limitations of coaching with colleagues

Two characteristics distinguish internal coaches from external ones:

- The internal coach is not truly independent with respect to the organisation.
- The internal coach has greater knowledge of the organisation within which (s)he practises.

There are different reasons – both fundamental and practical – for choosing internal or external coaches. There are also different possible ways of organising internal coaching, for example using a pool of coaches, or as an organisational function.

Opting for internal coaches has both advantages and limitations. These can be weighed up when choosing a coach in a specific situation.

Internal coaches can use all of the coaching approaches described in this book. In general, a directive approach appears to be quicker to apply in this context, especially in short-term coaching.

Internal coaches can make use of the codes of conduct for external coaches. They can use the same ethical framework with regard to:

- respect
- integrity and confidentiality
- responsibility
- professional conduct and conflicts of interest.

Appendix A

Personal coaching profile

This form can be completed after a coaching conversation, by you in the position of coach, but also by your coachee for you.

It is interesting to compare the two approaches – by completing the form yourself as the coach, for example, and asking your coachee to fill it in as well. Once the form has been completed you can consider together with your coachee:

- On what dimension did the coachee experience the best interventions?
- What are the coachee's expectations? Do they coincide with the coach's profile?

Indicate the coach's position on each dimension:

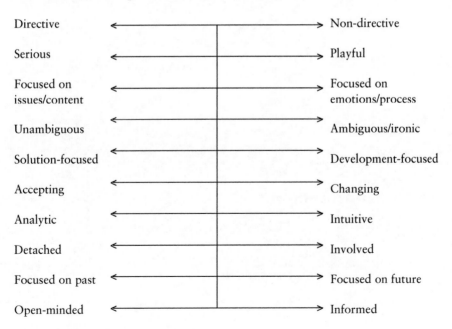

Directive	Non-directive
Serious	Playful
Focused on issues/content	Focused on emotions/process
Unambiguous	Ambiguous/ironic
Solution-focused	Development-focused
Accepting	Changing
Analytic	Intuitive
Detached	Involved
Focused on past	Focused on future
Open-minded	Informed

Appendix B

Verbatim exercise for the coach

One of the best ways to increase your professionalism as a coach is to reflect on how you are doing it now. It is difficult to gain an unbiased view of your own style of coaching. The following tool can help here, because it is based on the most literal representation of part of a coaching conversation. The exercise involves the verbatim – or word for word – exploration of a coaching session and comprises the following steps:

1. Record the first five to 15 minutes of a coaching conversation. Both video and audio recordings can be used.
2. Within a few days of the event, transcribe the tape recordings in the right-hand column using the following format:

Left hand column	*Right hand column*
....	....
....	....
....	....
....	....
....	....
....	....
....	....
	(literal text, including 'ums and ers')

This will quickly give you several pages of text.

3. In the left-hand column, write down thoughts and feelings of which you were aware during the conversation, as literally as possible.
4. Check the right-hand column text in terms of the following ingredients:
   a. Identify your own 'most-used' words; pay special attention to the use of words such as 'but', 'though', 'because', 'so', which – although short – express a clear intention.

b. Decide where on the scale of 'push' and 'pull' (see Appendix C) your own contributions are located.

c. Look at your own focus: what appears to be your primary concern here as the coach? (Examples: making contact, continuing to ask questions, applying structure, supporting, challenging, finding solutions ...)

d. What was the atmosphere like during the conversation and what indications of that atmosphere are there in the 'verbatim' text?

5. Have your own coach or supervisor read and comment on the 'verbatim' text. Look together at the links and tensions between left- and right-hand columns. How much did you use your own internal responses (in your left-hand column) to inform your interventions?

Appendix C
The sliding scale of 'push' and 'pull'

Coaching is really only possible with a strong and personal contact between yourself and the other person. You vary in the extent to which you as the coach or the other person as the coachee are at the centre. It is useful to be aware of this sliding scale between yourself and the other person, which runs from strict and clearly 'directive' to warm, attentive and 'non-directive' or, in other words, from 'push' to 'pull'.

Pull   Push   Making clear what you want and what you want to talk about.
Example: 'Listen, I would like to discuss your latest results.'

Pull   Push   Giving the other person an opinion or personal feedback.
Example: 'I think you're good at meeting almost impossible deadlines. I'm also pleased to see you so enthusiastic.'

Pull   Push   Associating with the other person's input, and revealing something of yourself that is triggered by that input.
Example: 'That makes me think of my time at Planning and Control, two years ago ...'

Pull   Push   Continuing with closed questions, or leading questions.
Example: 'Yes, but I am curious about what you did exactly. Did you or didn't you go to the manager?'

Pull   Push   Continuing with directive open questions.
Example: 'And what did you do once all of the figures were in?'

Pull   Push   Continuing with clarifying, 'pulling', open questions.
Example: 'Could you say more about what you mean by "analysing"?'

Pull   Push   'Reflecting' the other person: contributing your own here-and-now experience.
Example: 'Do you know, the way in which you talk about it is giving me a feeling of powerlessness now myself.'

Pull   Push Giving a summary of content and meaning for the other person.
                    Example: 'You say that you would like to start all over again,
                    and I notice that you're disappointed with the way things have
                    turned out.'

Pull   Push Giving a summary by literally repeating what the other person says.
                    Example: 'Think it through again ...?'

Pull   Push Listening with concentration, and occasionally encouraging the
                    other person to continue with a gesture or 'mmm'.
                    Example: ' ... '

Appendix D

Person-centred reflection form[1]

This form can be used just after a counselling conversation. It can help to deepen your contact with your coachee and to put your coachee more at the centre of the coaching conversation.

1. Contact

- Did you have contact with the coachee?
- Did you feel connected with the coachee?
- If not, was that because of you? Your coachee? The situation? Or ...?

2. Being accepted

- Were you accepted by your coachee?
- What evidence of that did you see in the coachee?
- What evidence of that did you perceive in yourself?
- How could you become more accepted?

3. Unconditional positive regard

- What associations did you have with regard to this coachee?
- Did you make assumptions about the coachee?
- Did you give the coachee directions or guidance?
- Was there any particular issue or situation that led you to feel less confidence in the coachee?
- Did you have the feeling that the coachee expected something of you? If so, what? What was your response?

---

1. Inspired by a feedback form used by Maggie Ridgewell and Jonathan Rosen of the Metanoia Institute, London.

4. *Empathy*

- Did you manage to move within your coachee's frame of reference?
- How do you think the coachee felt during the conversation?
- Did you interpret the coachee's question or want to solve the problem?
- Did you stay in strong contact with yourself?

5. *Congruence*

- What were the things that you did not say? That you found difficult to say?
- What did you find difficult to do?
- Was there something preventing you from just being yourself?
- What physical sensations did you notice in yourself? What emotions?
- What did you criticise in yourself?
- Did you disclose anything about yourself? If so, what was your coachee's response?

Appendix E

Coaching behaviours questionnaire[1]

This is the coach's version of the Ashridge Coaching Behaviours Survey, presented as a self-assessment exercise.

Introduction
This questionnaire has been designed to help you to assess your interventions as a coach. It lists a number of different ways in which you might act towards people, and asks you to think about how often you act in each of these ways.

Instructions
Listed below are many different ways in which you might act towards people in a coaching role. For each item, please indicate your perception of how often you act in that way in the right-hand box. None of these behaviours are good or bad in themselves – there are no 'right' or 'wrong' answers. You will get the most value from this exercise by being completely honest with yourself. Don't spend too long considering your replies: your immediate spontaneous answer is likely to be the most appropriate one.

If you find it difficult to give just one answer to a question (perhaps because you consider that you act differently towards different people) we suggest that you try to give an 'average answer' on this form. You may then want to raise this issue for discussion at a review with your own coach or supervisor.

When answering the questions:
0 – Not at all (or 'not applicable')
1 – Rarely
2 – Sometimes, but not often
3 – Moderately often
4 – Often
5 – Very often

1. This questionnaire has been developed by Richard Phillips at Ashridge, based on the six categories of counselling intervention that John Heron (1975) has proposed. We are grateful for Richard's help in publishing his questionnaire.

'When working with people as a coach, I tend to do the following':

Question		Your reply
0	*Example answer: please fill in your replies in this box* ⟶	1-5
1	advise them of the appropriate action to take	
2	explain the purpose of a task	
3	raise their awareness of their own learning needs	
4	ask them to tell me about a negative incident which they have experienced	
5	encourage them to set their own learning goals	
6	show my respect for them as individuals	
7	give them feedback about the impact of their behaviour	
8	invite them to talk about a difficult personal experience of theirs	
9	help them to reflect on their experiences	
10	express my concern to help them	
11	suggest that they choose a particular solution	
12	inform them about a learning opportunity	
13	ask them what they have learnt from a particular incident	
14	acknowledge the value of their ideas, beliefs, opinions	
15	persuade them to take a particular approach	
16	interpret their experiences or behaviour	
17	ask questions to uncover what they are hiding or avoiding	
18	encourage them to express their emotions	
19	apologise for anything I do which is unfair, forgetful, hurtful	
20	ask them how they can apply what they have learnt	
21	help them to recognise their own emotions	
22	challenge their denials or defensiveness	
23	make them aware of the choices open to them	
24	ask that they change their behaviour	
25	ask them how they feel about a success which they achieved	
26	make them aware of their mistakes	
27	offer them an explanation of what has happened	
28	inform them about the criteria for measuring success in performing a task	

29	ask open questions to promote discovery	
30	praise them for a job well done	
31	encourage them to find their own solutions and answers	
32	ask them why they are upset or angry	
33	offer them emotional support in difficult times	
34	present facts which contradict their opinions	
35	demonstrate skills or actions that I want them to copy	
36	give them information which they need to achieve a task	
37	draw their attention to facts which they have missed	
38	reflect their feelings by describing what I see in their behaviour	
39	make them feel welcome when they visit me	
40	recommend the best way to do something	
41	challenge their assumptions	
42	ask them to evaluate their own performance	
43	give them feedback about their results	
44	propose the best course of action for them to take	
45	ask them to express feelings which are blocking their progress	
46	show them the consequences of their actions	
47	ask them to set their own work objectives and targets	
48	make myself accessible to them when needed	
49	help them 'with my hands in my pockets': i.e. without interfering	
50	ask them how they feel about a current difficulty	
51	encourage them to feel good about themselves	
52	tell them where to go to find information and help	
53	show them how to correct their mistakes	
54	confront issues of poor performance	
55	tell them how to get started on a new task	
56	reveal information about my own experiences	
57	affirm positive qualities or actions of theirs which they are denying	
58	help them to express their insights after an emotional experience	
59	help them to map out their present understanding	
60	share information about my own failures and weaknesses	

Record the score corresponding to the item number (1–60) in the appropriate spaces indicated below. Total each row to get your final score for each of the six behavioural styles of coaches.

1.:	2.:	3.:	4.:	5.:	6.: ......
11.:	12.:	7.:	8.:	9.:	10.: ......
15.:	16.:	17.:	18.:	13.:	14.: ......
24.:	23.:	22.:	21.:	20.:	19.: ......
28.:	27.:	26.:	25.:	29.:	30.: ......
35.:	36.:	34.:	32.:	31.:	33.: ......
40.:	37.:	41.:	38.:	42.:	39.: ......
44.:	43.:	46.:	45.:	47.:	48.: ......
53.:	52.:	54.:	50.:	49.:	51.: ......
55.:	56.:	57.:	58.:	59.:	60.: ......
DR:	IN:	CH:	RE:	DI:	SU: ......

DR   directing (Heron's prescriptive interventions)
IN   informing (Heron's informative interventions)
CH   challenging (Heron's confronting interventions)
RE   releasing (Heron's cathartic interventions)
DI   discovering (Heron's catalytic interventions)
SU   supporting (Heron's supportive interventions)

Like the Personal Coaching Profile in Appendix A, this is an excellent tool for comparing your own scores with those of your coachee. You can then ask your coachee to complete the Coaching Behaviour Questionnaire with regard to yourself, both in terms of your most prominent behavioural styles and of what the coachee would like to see more or less of. At Ashridge Consulting we have available appropriate questionnaires for coachees, as well as interpretation software and a database of 600 coaches with which to make comparisons.

Bibliography

Argyris, C. (1990). *Overcoming Organizational Defenses: facilitating organizational learning*. Englewood Cliffs, N.J.: Prentice-Hall.

Armstrong, D. (1997). The 'institution in the mind': reflections on the relation of psycho-analysis to work with institutions. *Free Associations* 7.41, pp. 1–14.

Arthur, M.B. (1994). The boundaryless career: a new perspective for organizational inquiry. *Journal of Organizational Behaviour* 15.4, pp. 295–306.

Beutler, L.E., Crago, M. and Arizmendi, T.G. (1986). Therapist variables in psychotherapy process and outcome. In: *Handbook of Psychotherapy and Behavior Change*, 3rd Edition (eds S.L. Garfield and A.E. Bergin), pp. 257–310. New York: Wiley.

Beutler, L.E., Machado, P.P. and Allstetter Neufeldt, S. (1994). Therapist variables. In: *Handbook of Psychotherapy and Behavior Change*, 4th Edition (eds S.L. Garfield and A.E. Bergin), pp. 229–69. New York: Wiley.

Bion, W.R. (1961). *Experiences in Groups*. London: Tavistock.

Bion, W.R. (1962). *Learning from Experience*. London: William Heinemann.

Bion, W.R. (1963). *Elements of Psychoanalysis*. London: William Heinemann.

Bion, W.R. (1965). *Transformations*. London: William Heinemann.

Bion, W.R. (1970). *Attention and Interpretation*. London: Tavistock.

Breuer, J. and Freud, S. (1895). *Studien über Hysterie*. Leipzig/Vienna: Verlag Franz Deuticke. Translated as *Studies on Hysteria* by James Strachey in collaboration with Anna Freud in *The Standard Edition of the Complete Psychological Works of Sigmund Freud*, Volume II.

Brown, D. and Pedder, J. (1979). *Introduction to Psychotherapy*. London: Tavistock.

Cooperrider, D.L. and Srivastva, S. (1987). Appreciative inquiry in organizational life. In: *Research in Organizational Change and Development* 1 (eds W.A. Pasmore and R.W. Woodman), pp. 129–69. Greenwich, Conn.: JAI Press.

Cooperrider, D.L. and Whitney, D.L. (2002). *Appreciative Inquiry: the handbook*. Euclid, Ohio: Lakeshore.

Corsini, R.J. and Wedding, D. (1989). *Current Psychotherapies*. Ithasca, Ill.: Peacock.

Czander, W.M. (1993). *The Psychodynamics of Work and Organizations*. New York: Guilford Press.

De Board, R. (1978). *The Psychoanalysis of Organizations*. London: Routledge.

de Haan, E. (1994). *Contributions to Vision Research*. University of Utrecht, Ph.D. thesis.

de Haan, E. (1999). Weldadig spreken met dubbele tong: ironie als techniek van de helpende buitenstaander bij veranderingen [Speaking helpfully with a 'double tongue': irony as a technique of the helping outsider in change]. *Filosofie in Bedrijf* 34, pp. 54–64.

de Haan, E. (2004). *Learning with Colleagues: an action guide for peer consultation*. Basingstoke, UK: Palgrave Macmillan.

De Jong, P. and Berg, I.K. (2001). *Interviewing for Solutions*. Florence, Ky.: Wadsworth.

De Shazer, S. (1985). *Keys to Solution in Brief Therapy*. New York: Norton.

Downey, M. (1999). *Effective Coaching*. New York: Thomson Texere.

Dumont, F. (1991). Expertise in psychotherapy: inherent liabilities of becoming experienced. *Psychotherapy* 28, pp. 422–8.

Erickson, M.H. (1959). Further clinical techniques of hypnosis: utilization techniques. *American Journal of Clinical Hypnosis* 2, pp. 3–21.

Farrelly, F., and Brandsma, J. (1974). *Provocative Therapy*. Cupertino, Calif.: Meta.

Freud, A. (1936). *Das Ich und die Abwehrmechanismen*. Vienna: Internationaler Psychoanalytischer Verlag. Translated as *The Ego and the Mechanisms of Defence* by Cecil Baines. London: Hogarth.

Freud, S. (1894). Die Abwehr-Neuropsychosen. *Neurologisches Zentralblatt* 10 and 11. Translated as *The Neuro-Psychoses of Defence* by James Strachey in collaboration with Anna Freud in *The Standard Edition of the Complete Psychological Works of Sigmund Freud*, Volume III, pp. 45–61.

Freud, S. (1896). Weitere Bemerkungen über die Abwehr-Neuropsychosen. *Neurologisches Zentralblatt* 10. Translated as *Further Remarks on the Neuro-Psychoses of Defence* by James Strachey in collaboration with Anna Freud in *The Standard Edition of the Complete Psychological Works of Sigmund Freud*, Volume III, pp. 163–88.

Freud, S. (1900). *Die Traumdeutung*. Vienna: Verlag Franz Deuticke. Translated as *The Interpretation of Dreams* by James Strachey in collaboration with Anna Freud in *The Standard Edition of the Complete Psychological Works of Sigmund Freud*, Volumes IV and V.

Freud, S. (1904/1924). *Zur psychopathologie des Alltagslebens: 10. weiter vermehrte Auflage* (1924). Vienna: Internationale Psychoanalytische Verlag. Translated as *The Psychopathology of Everyday Life* by James Strachey in collaboration with Anna Freud in *The Standard*

Edition of the Complete Psychological Works of Sigmund Freud, Volume VI.

Freud, S. (1905). *Der Witz und seine Beziehung zum Unbewußten*. Vienna: Verlag Franz Deuticke. Translated as *Jokes and their Relation to the Unconscious* by James Strachey in collaboration with Anna Freud in *The Standard Edition of the Complete Psychological Works of Sigmund Freud*, Volume VIII.

Freud, S. (1912a). Die Handhabung der Traumdeutung in der Psychoanalyse. In: *Zentralblatt für Psychoanalyse*, Vol. II. Translated as *The Handling of Dream-Interpretation in Psycho-Analysis* by James Strachey in collaboration with Anna Freud in *The Standard Edition of the Complete Psychological Works of Sigmund Freud*, Volume XII, pp. 89–96.

Freud, S. (1912b). Zur Dynamik der Übertragung. *Zentralblatt für Psychoanalyse*, Vol. II. Translated as *The Dynamics of Transference* by James Strachey in collaboration with Anna Freud in *The Standard Edition of the Complete Psychological Works of Sigmund Freud*, Volume XII, pp. 97–108.

Freud, S. (1912c). Ratschläge für den Arzt bei der Psychoanalytischen Behandlung. *Zentralblatt für Psychoanalyse*, Vol. II. Translated as *Recommendations to Physicians Practising Psycho-Analysis* by James Strachey in collaboration with Anna Freud in *The Standard Edition of the Complete Psychological Works of Sigmund Freud* , Volume XII, pp. 109–20.

Freud, S. (1913). Zur Einleitung der Behandlung. *Internationale Zeitschrift für ärztliche Psychoanalyse*, Vol. I. Translated as *On Beginning the Treatment* by James Strachey in collaboration with Anna Freud in *The Standard Edition of the Complete Psychological Works of Sigmund Freud*, Volume XII, pp. 121–44.

Freud, S. (1914a). Erinnern, Wiederholen und Durcharbeiten. *Zeitschrift für Psychoanalyse*, Vol. II. Translated as *Remembering, Repeating and Working Through* by James Strachey in collaboration with Anna Freud in *The Standard Edition of the Complete Psychological Works of Sigmund Freud*, Volume XII, pp. 145–56.

Freud, S. (1914b). Der Moses des Michelangelo. *Imago*, Vol. III. Translated as *The Moses of Michelangelo* by James Strachey in collaboration with Anna Freud in *The Standard Edition of the Complete Psychological Works of Sigmund Freud*, Volume III, pp. 43–61.

Freud, S. (1915). Bemerkungen über die Übertragungsliebe. *Zeitschrift für Psychoanalyse*, Vol. III. Translated as *Observations on Transference-Love* by James Strachey in collaboration with Anna Freud in *The Standard Edition of the Complete Psychological Works of Sigmund Freud*, Volume XIII, pp. 211–40.

Freud, S. (1923). *Das Ich und das Es*. Leipzig/Vienna/Zürich: Internationaler psychoanalytischer Verlag. Translated as *The Ego and the Id* by James Strachey in collaboration with Anna Freud in *The Standard Edition of the Complete Psychological Works of Sigmund Freud*, Volume XIX, pp. 12–68.

Freud, S. (1925). Die Verneinung. *Imago*, Vol. XI. Translated as *Negation* by James Strachey in collaboration with Anna Freud in *The Standard Edition of the Complete Psychological Works of Sigmund Freud*, Volume XIX, pp. 235–42.

Freud, S. (1926). *Hemmung, Symptom und Angst*. Leipzig/Vienna/Zürich: Psychoanalytischer Verlag. Translated as *Inhibitions, Symptoms and Anxiety* by James Strachey in collaboration with Anna Freud in *The Standard Edition of the Complete Psychological Works of Sigmund Freud*, Volume XX, pp. 87–178.

Freud, S. (1928). Der Humor. *Imago*, Vol. XIV. Translated as *Humour* by James Strachey in collaboration with Anna Freud in *The Standard Edition of the Complete Psychological Works of Sigmund Freud*, Volume XXI, pp. 159–66.

Frisch, M.H. (2001). The emerging role of the internal coach. *Consulting Psychology Journal: practice and research* 53.4, pp. 240–50.

Gallwey, T. (1974). *The Inner Game of Tennis*. London: Jonathan Cape.

Gergen, K.J. (1999). *An Invitation to Social Construction*. London: Sage.

Goldfried, M.R., Greenberg, L.S. and Marmar, C. (1990). Individual psychotherapy: process and outcome. *Annual Review of Psychology* 41, pp. 659–88.

Haley, J. (1963). *Strategies of Psychotherapy*. New York: Grune and Stratton.

Hawkins, P. and Shohet, R. (2000). *Supervision in the Helping Professions – an individual, group and organizational approach*. Buckingham: Open University Press.

Hawton, K., Salkovskis, P.M., Kirk, J. and Clark, D.M. (1989). *Cognitive Behaviour Therapy for Psychiatric Problems: a practical guide*. Oxford: Oxford University Press.

Heimann, P. (1950). On counter-transference. *International Journal of Psychoanalysis* 31, pp. 81–4.

Heron, J. (1975). *Helping the Client*. London: Sage.

Homer (8th century BC). *The Odyssey*. Translated by E.V. Rieu. London: Penguin Classics (1946).

Kampa-Kokesch, S. and Anderson, M.Z. (2001). Executive coaching: a comprehensive review of the literature. *Consulting Psychology Journal: Practice and Research* 53.4, pp. 205–28.

Kanter, R.M. (1989). Careers and the wealth of nations: a macro-perspective on the structure and implications of career forms. In: *Handbook of Career Theory* (eds M.B. Arthur, D. Hall and B. Lawrence), pp. 506–21. New York: Cambridge University Press.

Klein, M. (1946) Notes on some schizoid mechanisms. *International Journal of Psychoanalysis* 27 pp. 99–109.

Kolb, D.A. (1984). *Experiential Learning: experience as the source of learning and development*. Englewood Cliffs, N.J.: Prentice-Hall.

Lambert, M.J. (1989). The individual therapist's contribution to psychotherapy process and outcome. *Clinical Psychology Review* 9, pp. 469–85.

Lambert, M.J. and Bergin, A.E. (1994). The effectiveness of psychotherapy. In: *Handbook of Psychotherapy and Behaviour Change*, 4th Edition (eds S.L. Garfield and A.E. Bergin), pp. 143–89. New York: Wiley.

Lapworth, P., Sills, C. and Fish, S. (2001). *Integration in Counselling and Psychotherapy: developing a personal approach*. London: Sage.

Lear, J. (2003). *Therapeutic Action: an earnest plea for irony*. London: Karnac.

Luft, J. (1969). *Of Human Interaction*. Palo Alto, Calif.: Mayfield.

Malan, D.H. (1995). *Individual Psychotherapy and the Science of Psychodynamics*. London: Butterworth Heinemann.

Maslow, A.H. (1962). *Towards a Psychology of Being*. Princeton, N.J.: Van Nostrand.

McGovern, J., Lindemann, M., Vergara, M., Murphy, S., Barker, L. and Warrenfeltz, R. (2001). Maximizing the impact of executive coaching: behavioural change, organizational outcomes, and return on investment. *Manchester Review* 6.1, pp. 1–9.

McNeal, B.W., May, R.J. and Lee, V.E. (1987). Perceptions of counsellor source characteristics by premature and successful terminators. *Journal of Counselling Psychology* 34, pp. 86–9.

Mehrabian, A. (1972). *Nonverbal Communication*. Chicago: Aldine-Atherton.

Olivero, G., Bane, K.D. and Kopelman, R.E. (1997). Executive coaching as a transfer of training tool: effects on productivity in a public agency. *Public Personnel Management* 26.4, pp. 461–9.

Patterson, C.H. (1987). Comments. *Person-Centered Review* 1, pp. 246–8.

Peltier, B. (2001) *The Psychology of Executive Coaching: theory and application*. New York: Brunner and Routledge.

Ragins, B.R., Cotton, J.L. and Miller, J.S. (2000). Marginal mentoring: the effects of type of mentor, quality of relationship, and program design on work and career attitudes. *Academy of Management Journal* 43.6, pp. 1177–94.

Raskin, N.J. (1952). An objective study of the locus-of-evaluation factor in psychotherapy. In: *Success in Psychotherapy*, (eds W. Wolff and J.A. Precker), pp. 143–62. New York: Grune and Stratton.

Reed, B.D. (2000). *An Exploration of Role*. London: Grubb Institute.

Rogers, C.R. (1957). The necessary and sufficient conditions of therapeutic personality change. *Journal of Consulting Psychology* 21, pp. 95–103.

Rogers, C.R. (1961). *On Becoming a Person: a therapist's view of psychotherapy*. London: Constable.

Rogers, C.R. (1970). *Carl Rogers on Encounter Groups*. New York: Harper and Row.

Roth, A. and Fonagy, P. (1996). *What Works For Whom? A critical review of psychotherapy research*. London: Guildford.

Schulz von Thun, F. (1982). *Miteinander reden* [Talking together]. Reinbek bei Hamburg: Rowohlt.

Schutz, W.C. (1958). *FIRO: a three-dimensional theory of interpersonal behaviour*. New York: Rinehart.

Senge, P.M., Kleiner, A., Roberts, C., Ross, R.B. and Smith, B.J. (1994). *The Fifth Discipline Fieldbook: strategies and tools for building a learning organization*. London: Nicholas Brealey.

Smither, J.W., London, M., Flautt, R., Vargas, Y, Kucine, I. (2003). Can working with an executive coach improve multisource feedback ratings over time? A quasi-experimental field study. *Personnel Psychology* 56, pp. 23–44.

Sue-Chan, C. and Latham, G.P. (2004). The relative effectiveness of external, peer and self-coaches. *Applied Psychology* 53.2, pp. 260–78.

Symington, N. (1986). *The Analytic Experience*. London: Free Association Books.

Twijnstra, A. and Keuning, D. (1988). *Organisatieadvieswerk* [The practice of organisation consulting]. Leiden, the Netherlands: Stenfert Kroese.

Vaillant, G.E. (1992). *Ego Mechanisms of Defense: a guide for clinicians and researchers*. Washington D.C.: American Psychiatric Press.

Wasylyshyn, K.M. (2003). Executive coaching: an outcome study. *Consulting Psychology Journal: Practice and Research* 55.2, pp. 94–106.

Watzlawick, P., Beavin, J., and Jackson, D.D. (1967). *Pragmatics of Human Communication*. New York: W.W. Norton.

Weick, K.E. (1995). *Sensemaking in Organizations*. London: Sage.

Whitmore, J. (1992). *Coaching for Performance: GROWing people, performance and purpose*. Nicholas Brealey Publishing, London.

Yalom, I.D. (1992). *When Nietzsche Wept*. New York: HarperCollins.

Index